THANKH YOU

I Am ThAnkhful for the all, the Oneness. Mind, Body, and Spirit. I would like to give Thankhs to my Earth Parents whom portal I chose to come through in this dimension. My loving mother I thank you unconditionally, you did an excellent job raising me. The Gods and other Goddesses with whom I share this experience. If you were ever apart of my movie, I ThAnkh you.

Love, Light, Truth and Prosperity to my Royal Creations, ALL my children. ThAnkhs to Chartima Mekia, aka Mama Kasmos.

DEDICATION

This book is dedicated to MyCellph (You); the many reflections of myself. Man, Woman and Child. I believe in me, we (Us). I am dedicated to helping raise the vibration of love.

TABLE OF CONTENTS

PORTAL

My mother stayed up all night gambling with my dad's family. Her, my grandmother Virginia and Aunts would all hang out and play card games. They would drink and listen to dusties (Old School R & B). She went into labor with me that morning. My stepdad Jamie drove her to Trinity hospital in Chicago. She gave me my real dad's first name and I don't know why because he wasn't at the hospital when I was born on January 24th, 1988. I have 3 older siblings. We all have different dads. My mother was always working. She worked full time at Navy Pier. Stayed on top of her business. They would describe her as built like a brickhouse. Meaning she was thick in all the right

1

places. We went to her job to participate in different activities they had all year round. She had been working there for years. When my mother was not at work, she was at bingo with my grandma and their homegirls at 369 in Indiana. I would stay over to my grandmother's house a lot growing up.

Thelma Lou bertha was my mother's mom who lived out south of Princeton St., at 300 W. 117th. It was roaches at my granny crib. I saw one crawl in her ear and mouth before. She used to sleep with her mouth open sitting upright in her green rocking chair. If you caught her sleeping, she would say "I'm not sleeping I'm resting my eyes." My grandmother was a wise old woman. It is where I got most of my wisdom. Thelma didn't take no stuff, was tougher than any old woman I have ever come across. Her heart was of gold.

She would let me go and help Mrs. Lapoint. She was the only white lady in a black neighborhood. Mrs. Lapoint would pull up in front of her home with her groceries. She lived in the home by herself. Eventually she started paying me, but I was just happy to help her carry them up her stairs. I had my bottle until I was 6 years old. My granny didn't care, I was her baby. One day, one of the younger guys who is older than me offered to give me $20 if I threw my bottle away. I tossed that bottle in the garbage and took that money so fast. I was crying when my granny came in from bingo that night. She was yelling at the whole house to go and get me a bottle. It was late so whoever got it had to walk to 119th store and buy me a new one. I always had fun at grandma house. I would ride my bike over there, everyone knew what family I belonged to.

Everyone in the neighborhood all knew each other. My grandma had 6 children, and my mother was the only girl. So, I didn't have a big family. I started hanging with the kids across the street from my grandma's house, since I visited often. They were my first friends. It was so many of them that we just started calling each other cousins. I was the oldest of course, and for the most part we were a bunch of tomboys who would play double dutch. Whenever I wasn't at home with my mom, or with granny, I was usually across the street with the other kids. Their granny would babysit me sometimes. One day this she made us go pick our switches off the tree. Lily Mae didn't play at all, she would give us a down south whooping. If we didn't pick a thick switch, she would tell us to go pick another one.

My grandma Thelma stayed back to watch the children one day while the other ladies went to bingo. I was sitting at the table in the kitchen because she was cooking, and I was hungry. To my surprise she cooked something called liver, and rice. I had never eaten that before or heard of it! I tossed it into the ashtray she had sitting on the table, that she hadn't yet removed. My granny took one look at me and scurried to the table took the liver out the ashtray and shoved it into my mouth so hard it was in my throat. I was mad but what could I do, homie didn't play that.

We went back to our house on 72nd and Emerald. It had been a couple days since I had gone out south to the 100's. Instead I went to the neighbor's house behind where we lived on emerald. We were watching tv at first, then me looking for something on the floor caused him to crawl behind me. We were both hands and knees crawling on the floor until he wouldn't back up. The lil boy was head butting me, literally. Next thing I know I'm sitting on the couch and can't move until my mom came. Man listen, when we got home my mother put me in the tub, dried me off and oiled me down really good and whooped my butt with a belt. I didn't even know why I was getting a whopping. I was just trying to move the boy head off my butt.

I started spending more time at home. I wasn't sure if it was because school was starting, and I was starting Kindergarten. The first school I attended was William A. Hinton on 71st. My mother had seen one of the young boys from the neighborhood walking to school and asked if I could walk with him. He agreed, and to school we walked. The first bell had just rung for all the students to be in the building just as I was about to walk in the school building. The teacher was standing at the door collecting report cards as we are walking inside. My feet barely touched the step to go inside as I immediately realized my mother didn't sign my report card. I turned around and ran back to my house as if I was running a marathon and didn't stop until I made it back to our house. My mother couldn't believe I ran back home. After school I was running through her walk-through closet. My mother always dressed nice and she used to drive a green thunderbird, the color of her birthstone. The way I was raised I knew we came from money.

My grandmother got sick, so I went to live with this lady named Lil bit in Chicago Heights. I didn't know why I was going with this lady that I didn't know, with no explanation as to why. She had to have been my guardian at the time because she enrolled me in school. My siblings or none of the familiar faces I knew was around. I felt so out of place, abandoned even. *Who is this lady and where is my mother I remember thinking?*

One day after school a group of kids were bullying me. As far as I know the kids were bullying me about my mother not wanting me. I ran as they chased me all the way to the block where I was staying at the time with Lil bit. I did not like being at her home. I did not feel loved at all. My plate had to be clear before I could get anything to drink. If I didn't eat all my food that was placed onto my plate, I had to go to bed thirsty.

It didn't take long for me to catch on. I would put peas and other vegetables into a napkin and throw it in the garbage. After pretending to eat my food, it was time to shower and get ready for bed. Lil bit told me to go put my dirty clothes in the dryer. Being a kid, I turned the knob on the dryer, and it started. She heard the dryer going and I was getting a whooping with a belt within a matter of milliseconds. I heard her saying "I didn't tell you to touch nothing."

It had been maybe a month maybe two, before I reunited back with my mother. I was happy to be back with her. We had relocated to another home, and my grandmother Thelma was there, in a hospital bed. She had four huge oxygen tanks hooked up to her. My mother had to assist my granny because she was diagnosed with colon cancer. My mother had to handle all of my granny important business. My granny apartment was being worked on, her bills, plus relocating our home from Emerald to 72nd and Perry. It had been a couple nights since I was back. Even though my granny was in the hospital bed and gown, she looked fine. She was smiling and kissing me still breathing and enjoying life. That night she did not wake up.

GIFT OF GAB

I went over to Jamie's house. He helped take care of me even though I wasn't his biological daughter. For a while I thought he was my dad. Often times my mom would pull up to his home on Eggleston. We would walk up to the building and then go in on the enclosed front porch and ring the doorbell. My dad had a room inside this home. The woman had a candy store in her kitchen. I loved going to visit him, that house and the lady with the candy store. We would go upstairs to his bedroom. I heard my mom and dad talking but I didn't quite get what was going on. I was young so I was just there. Sitting in the chair beside his bed. I would just see his frustrations, and the look on his face before he handed her money. He hugged me and was gone until the next appearance.

They both played in the bowling league at the bowling alley located on 123rd and Halsted. I loved going there. It was a little playroom for all the kids who parents were in the bowling league. It was video games, and food at the Halsted St. bowling alley. Familiar with the other kids who came just as often as I did.

One time I caught pneumonia; I was like 10. My mom pulled up to the house that I enjoyed visiting, but this time I felt like crap. I was puking in the garbage can and farting at the same time. Diarrhea was just about to come out as my dad came to the door. I ran up the stairs and straight to the bathroom. The toilet was my seat until my mom was ready to go.

My mother was laid off from Navy Pier. I moved in with my sister Michelle, in Calumet City. We lived at 5 157th St., a block away from the Indiana state lines. My sister has a daughter, and we all lived in a 1-bedroom upstairs apartment. I attended fourth and fifth grade at Lincoln Elementary. I remember having recess at Lincoln. That was the only time I really got to link with the other kids my age from the other classrooms. It was a lot going on at that school. The first time I had been where it was so much diversity.

My mother would take my niece Kyree and I to go to the bingo hall with her. She went early in the day, hours before the games were to start. Her buddy who worked at the bingo hall would let her come get some bingo packets. My mom made us get donuts to distract us from what she was doing. We loved to go with her to the bingo hall and knew we would always get a treat. Bingo sounded like fun to me, you get to snack and win money. Kids were not allowed to play. Bingo was considered gambling. One day her old white friend she would get the bingo boards from touched my breast, it was so uncomfortable. I didn't know what was going on, and I never said anything to my mom.

Michelle worked at Amoco gas station, but it was in Chicago. It was about a 30minute drive from where we lived in Calumet. Kyree went with her dads' side of the family sometimes. My mom and I would get dressed and go out to the hundreds. My mom used to live off 105th and State St. She had friends and family in the neighborhood. We would post up for days at a time.

I loved being at my brother Adonis granny's house. His dad Brumo wasn't there that often. Ms. Brumfield was a sweetheart. She had a poodle dog named Benji. It is something about being around someone who has more experience than you. I considered older people to be wise. Grandma Brumfield gave a lot of love. My mom and I had our own space in the basement.

After a few days I went over to my moms' friend house Sandy. Sandy had five kids, all boys. I hung out with the boys that summer. We walked down to Cone school and played on the playground. Even when I wasn't with them, I was somewhere around the area playing with other children in the neighborhood. My mom's other friend lived on the next block, so it was a bunch of kids running around.

Catching lightening bugs, riding bikes, I was even wearing four-wheel skates now. Not the little kid ones you wear when you slide your feet in the front and back part with your shoe on. Basketball was played with a brown or orange crate tied to the tree in the back yard by the alley. Playing with fire, hide and seek, four corners. That was a lot of fun, rock teacher was one of my favorites.

They had a big family, and they all stayed in one house. It was so much fun over there. We were allowed to be kids. It was all boys too, so I really got away with anything. It was another cousin they had named lil Shine. He looked exactly like his dad, but big Shine had a big beard. The meals were always big, because it was a lot of us kids mainly.

We would all come in from outside playing. After we let the mosquitoes bite us until we had clusters of bites and scratching. The boys and I would prepare for dinner, washing our hands and lining up for our plates one by one. Sitting down wherever there was a seat. Once done with our food, their grandma Ms. Scotch made us wash our dishes and clean up after ourselves. Then, we all scattered all throughout the house. Some was upstairs in the room playing video games, the rest of us was downstairs watching television on a pallet.

Eventually I went to sleep. I woke up because I felt I had to use the bathroom. All the lights were off, and it was dark in the front room. I felt the energy from the television being on. The volume was turned down really low. They had central air, so I was chilly on the floor. I remember before I could even move my body, I felt something. I laid there pretending to still be sleep as if I was dreaming. I felt it again, it was a touch on my butt. *Was I being molested?*

I couldn't sleep that night. I was afraid Pee Wee would touch me again. I couldn't wait until morning to tell my mom. It was not like me to not eat. My sleep was interrupted, and with me barely sleeping I slept longer then all the other kids. They had already started eating. I gathered myself together, skipping breakfast and still replaying what had happened in my head. His own daughter was over that day. *Did he touch her too?*

When I walked in the door it was like my mother knew something was not right. I don't vividly remember the conversation. I just know she was furious. I could feel the fumes coming off of her as she got herself dressed and left. Not sure if my mom even approached him about it. I pictured her going around to their house giving him a mouth full of words that assured him I told. All I know is I never went back around that corner, and it took her a while to come back. I stayed at granny Brumfield house and sat on the front porch with her and Benji. I played with the girls that were next door and across from granny's house.

IMMACULATE

It was my 12th bearthday. I didn't go to school that Monday. My mom left me with my brother's girlfriend Paige. She would always smoke weed. One day she asked did I want to smoke. Paige held the blunt to my lips because she knew if my brother came in, he would be able to tell I had been smoking and would want to smell my figure tips. Sure, enough he did exactly that. Paige and I just looked at each other and laughed when he went out the bedroom.

My mom took me to her friend house, Jeryl. He worked as a male nurse. One night I was at Jeryl house on the air mattress in the hallway. I was sleep, but I woke up to my mom making these weird noises from the bedroom. It took me awhile to fall back to sleep. Spring break was coming up, and his family planned a trip to go to Las Vegas to see his brother and his family. It was my first time ever flying on an airplane. My mom or Jeryl didn't go. I went with his sister, aunt, niece, nephews, and cousins. We were deep with a lot of kids. I see my mom get smaller and smaller in the window waving as the plane took off.

Our stay was beyond fun at the Adventure dome theme park inside the Circus hotel across from the M&M and Coca Cola buildings. We spent a day or two with their family that lived in Vegas. I was excited about the indoor amusement park. I had met a guy whose bearthday was the same day as mine, but he was a few years older than me. He and his cousin were with their grandparents. We met up a few times inside the hotel, their rooms were closer to where the casino was inside. I found out that he and his cousin was from the same area we were from in Chicago, and we talked about linking outside of Vegas. The hotel was huge, we would get on the elevator, which would turn into a train. We would come out on the other side to a whole bunch of restaurants. We stayed in Vegas for about a week.

After we made it back to Chicago, I stayed at the house with Jeryl sister until my mom came and picked me up. His niece Tina had an extra bed in her bedroom that I would sleep in. I was laying down sleep, but I felt her touching me. Tina was feeling all on my chest and touching my private area. I pretended to be sleep, and before I knew it, she was on top of me dry humping me. At first, I was confused as to what she was doing and then it started feeling good in my private area. I just let her keep going. Tina was a few years older than me. She directed me to do the same thing to her and I experienced my first climax. As I kept going over there, she continued to wake me up in the middle of the night and eventually I didn't want to go over there anymore. It was getting annoying for her to wake me up out of my sleep. If I knew my mom was going over there, I would ask to go somewhere else.

We moved to a new crib on 64th and Evans. I had a crush on this dude Lil Ron across the street from where we lived. He had a girlfriend who would come visit him all the time. It was his girlfriend from around his old house before he moved across the street from us. Eventually, she stopped coming over. Lil Ron told me her dad made her stop seeing him because he was a couple years older.

Later in 2000 I lost my virginity. All the kids were down in the parking lot playing. I called Lil Ron across the street to our apartment building. We had already talked about this, so he knew I was ready. I walked upstairs to our door and he followed me in. He laid down on the chaise and directed me to get on top of him. I did as was told but it hurt. I kept sitting down and heard a pop. After a few seconds it didn't hurt as much, and we kept going until he was done. We both went back outside like nothing happen.

My mom came home about 30 mins later and I got the shit slapped out me for being outside. The slap didn't hurt as bad as being embarrassed, plus I was still dealing with the slight pain in my yoni. She made me sit on the floor on a pallet in the living room. I was moving around because it was very uncomfortable. We sat and watched tv for a while. Once I noticed my mom was doing her thang up drinking beer, I decided to tell her what I had done. I got up and walked in the kitchen to tell her that I had sex. Instead of me getting a whooping, nothing happened. She continued to do what she was doing before I walked into the kitchen. I didn't get a lecture, no rules, dos or don'ts. Shortly after that I started cutting my wrist, but I never let no one know. No one ever seen it either.

I dated Lil Ron for a year. His family was super cool. They always thought about me whenever they were doing stuff. They moved to a new house about 15 blocks away. I would catch the bus down cottage grove to his house on the weekends. When they were going to the movies, they called me and asked if I wanted to go. Lil Ron and I would sit on the phone to wee hours in the morning, sometimes until the birds were chirping. Listening to "You got it bad" by Usher or "Differences" by Ginuwine.

His parents allowed me to come over, but they didn't want us in the bedroom, especially with the door closed. We would watch movies or listen to music. He found a way for us to get a quick lovemaking in. Most times I would visit and go home, other days I would chill with his family. Sometimes we would have sex and cuddle. My family didn't understand what I seen in him. He had a cocked eye, from a bad science project that went wrong before he moved in my neighborhood. He was so sweet to me that it didn't bother me. I saw him for who he is.

It was a new pair of Jordan's that came out and his whole family had a pair. He thought of me and bought me a pair. It was the first time a guy had bought me anything. I knew he would because he had his sister ask my size. A pair of Retro 1 Silver Anniversary Jordan's. We were matching and I thought it was the cutest shit ever.

I had been dating Lil Ron outside of school and had a boyfriend in school. Dre was a varsity basketball player, and I was a starting cheerleader. One day Lil Ron got on the bus to come visit me and surprise me after school. I was stuck looking crazy to see him at the school. We broke up after that, and I ended up moving to Iowa after my 8th grade graduation.

PASSION

I was always late for work and got fired because of late attendance. Had been going to the alternative school, and the buses would only come every hour. Nothing like back home in Chicago where buses come every 15 mins. I started selling weed. All the school kids were smoking from me. Always been about my money. After a couple months of doing that I dropped out of school and decided to move back to Chicago that summer of 2005. I planned to go to the Community College. Instead I was just hanging out in the streets with drug dealers, smoking weed and not working or going to school.

My plan was to finish school out there and get a job. I stayed with Paige on 91st and Dobson. I hooked up with a married man a few times. My homegirl Jada introduced me to her cousin. I used to have sex with him, and he would give me money. That's how I got by for the duration of time living there. My homegirl was from the projects on 29th. We were having a good time one day, driving on the expressway headed from the 100's down to 29th to hang out with some of her peoples. I was in the backseat rolling up a blunt. She was driving and we had another homegirl with us sitting in the passenger, and I was in the back.

We were vibing and moving our head to whatever song was playing on 107.5 WGCI. All of a sudden, I got this feeling. I didn't know what it was, and as I went to light the blunt the generic crack head lighter wouldn't work. It was just working when I had smoked the cigarette. I tried to light the blunt the second time I noticed we were coming around a curve. I saw a white 18-wheeler semi-truck behind us literally less than a 500 ft away.

Jada had to be driving about 80mph. She tried to slow down, but lost control of the wheel and we started spinning. We did a whole 360 and a half degrees and managed to be facing the opposite way when the car finally stopped. The semitruck was even closer, all three of us hoped out the car and fmmmmmmm the sound of the semi-truck was just now flying pass us. The truck was behind our car just enough that it had time to switch lanes. The vehicle was a steamer, so we didn't call the police. We climbed up the expressway grassy hill to the main St.

We were able to call one of Jada homeboys named Geno, and he picked us up on 47th and State St. I had seen my life flash before my eyes. Once in the car, her homie immediately poured us some Remy. Jada said because it was my first time taking an ecstasy, she only gave me half of her half of pill. My teeth were grinding, and mouth was moving. I couldn't stop rubbing on myself. Jada was like five foot one, and size 0-1 but she was my big homie. We were making money, escorting services, private parties. I hung out with Jada, and met a few other people threw her. We stayed at this guy house one time. Jada and the other girls left to do a private party and I didn't go. The guy whose house we were at came in the room where I was sleeping and started having sex with me. I told Jada about it and we left, and I never seen him again.

Paige and I weren't getting along. I got everything I had there and packed it in one big laundry bag that they sell at the laundromats. Adonis lady friend said she would pick me up, but she never showed up. I was looking crazy standing on the bus stop too stubborn to go back to Paige house. It was about 5 o'clock in the evening when three light skinned dudes pulled up in a dark blue four door car. They asked if I needed a ride and I hopped in with them, laundry bag included. We went to one of the guys cribs. His mom wasn't there. He offered me a soda, some food and told me to make myself comfortable as he gestured to the refrigerator for me to get it myself. When I looked in the refrigerator, I noticed a picture of him and his mom. The dudes were a couple years older than me, so I assumed they were attending college.

They were talking about a dorm party in Joliet. We made a stop at the store, then kicked it in the area for a while. Around 8 o'clock we headed to the expressway. At the dorm people start showing up, music was playing, and everyone had a red plastic cup. I don't

24

know if I was drugged or not, but somehow, I exchanged energy with two of the three dudes. The last one tried but I noticed what was happening and he didn't get a chance. The guys went to drop some of the people off who didn't live on campus. I got in the shower and cleaned myself.

Hours had passed and I was left at this dorm by myself. I went to sleep that night and the next day was hungry when I got up. It was no food in the refrigerator, like no one lived there. It was a packet of oatmeal, so I made that. Waited all day for someone to show up. No one arrived. Another night in this dorm. I have to figure out something, *they left me here*. I thought to myself. The next day I decided to leave, and I didn't know where I was going. My prepaid phone was off, and I had no money. I walked outside the campus dorm room and knocked on a couple doors. One door opened and it was a guy. I asked if I could use his phone. He could sense my energy because he ended up giving me money for a Metra train ticket and something to eat. That was the day I knew I had to save myself.

I started hanging on Princeton more. I hooked up with Byrd, he was one of the younger guys from the area. We hung out talking shit, joking around and smoking weed. Listening to music and driving around most days. One day Byrd and I were talking, and the white part of his eyes were brown and cloudy. I thought it was strange. Talked to my mom over the phone. She was still in Iowa. The conversation was short. I called to let her know I missed her and was ready to come home. I asked if her can you see death in someone's eyes. She told me you could.

A few days later my homie from Iowa Luke was in Chicago. He told me he was going to Iowa soon. I wanted to ride back with him. I was ready to leave Chicago on my own this time. I was giving Paige money to live with her. Our hot water didn't work. We had to warm up pots of water on the stove to make bathwater. It was so hot that summer we would even take cold showers sometimes. I ended up missing my ride to Iowa. Next time I spoke with Luke he was already in Iowa. He told me he was with someone I wanted to talk to, then Von got on the phone. We talked briefly about when I come back, so I was excited. I arrived in Iowa on the greyhound bus a couple days later.

I met Von at 16. He would let me drive his 4-door grey car to school. He is 7 years older than me, so we were just hanging out. I practically had my own crib. My mother was never home, it was work or her boyfriend house. Somedays I would not even get up, I would sleep in. She worked third shift. Once she noticed I was doing that she would come after her shift and make sure I was up. One time, Von was released from the county jail to go to BEP, which is a batterers education program. Instead he came to my house, with his shoestrings in his hand. He the reason they eventually stopped releasing people and made the class in jail. I told him I would see him later.

I was happy to be back in Iowa for some reason. Paige called not even a week later to tell me that Byrd had been killed sitting in his car. I couldn't believe it. *Did I really see that in his eyes?* That was my dawg. Von and I became inseparable. Doing everything together. If you see me, you seen him. We became a great team. I was 18 so I was ok with us dating. We lived with his sisters for a while. I used his younger sister ID to start dancing at the gentlemen's club. Diamond Girls was where his suns mother Mila worked. She had enough plug to get me in there. My stage name was Passion.

Mila allowed me into her home, and I watched her children somedays when she worked. She went out of town one day with her dancing buddies. They were going to pick up some dudes in Rockford. When they came back, she let us know they were at her homegirl crib. Von and I dropped the babies off to her, but he left me there. The girls were talking about dancing that night, so I wanted to go back to Mila house up the hill to get my perm to do my hair. I wanted to be up to part if I was going to dance. After realizing I didn't have the house key on the keychain, I went back to Mila homegirl house. She mentioned Von came back and was looking for me. I went outside just as he was pulling up. He yelled at me to get in the car. He asked a question but before I could answer he backhanded me so hard that my head went down into the passenger seat, and my legs flew up towards the windshield.

I stayed with him after that. Praying to God to give me a baby. I felt like the emptiness I felt would go away. Von and I became pregnant on my birthday of 2006. I was happy that I was finally receiving what I prayed for. That summer we hung out with our friends all day long. We got our own house on 19ᵗʰ and Jackson. It was a 2 bedroom on Section 8. I would cook and our friends would come hang out and chill at our house. Von had trust issues, abusive and would accuse me of cheating. I remember one time we came from Church, Von called me the b word. I replied with, "you heard what the pastor said at church today, what you call your partner is what you are." One of his homeboys from Kankakee had come to visit. He slept in the second bedroom. I didn't want him to come, but Von was trying to help him out. He accused me of cheating with the dude. It made me so uncomfortable to be in my own home. The friend left and never came back.

The one accusing is the guilty one. When I was 6 months pregnant, I caught him in the hotel with my homegirl. It had been a long night, and I was tired. I had a beer at the birthday party we went to. My homegirl at the time rode along to drop me off. Von assured me he was coming back soon. I woke up in the middle of the night and he was not home. Panicking not knowing if he was in jail, or safe, I just knew he wasn't home, and it was 3 something in the morning. I called both of his phones, straight to voicemail.

Next, I called his sisters, they hadn't heard from him. We called the county he wasn't there. I called the last number of who I know he talked to prior to dropping me off. It was one of his female workers, and she said she hadn't seen him. A few minutes late she called back and asked, "Well who did I get the room for at the hotel?" The woman had gotten the room in her name. I was shaking at this point. She told me all the details over the phone, as she was driving to pick me up and take me to where Von was at. As soon as we pulled in the parking lot, I noticed my car. I had headphones under my shirt on the phone with his big sister, so you couldn't notice it. I only had one ear bud in.

The woman knocked on the door, after it was answered she moved to the side. Once opened I let off on both of them. Von was sleep but woke up to me beating him in his back yelling, "get the F***k up!" He stayed there that night, didn't come home for days. I begged him to come home. I forgave him, and when he did, he was so tired he was sleep for most of the day. I was outside with my other friends pretending to be having myself a good ole time. I was really worried about what he would say if he knew I had all the weed, the car, keys, and money. He ended up in jail that night and missed the birth of our sun.

I heard a knock at the door when I made it back home after giving birth. It was just the baby and I, and I wasn't expecting any visitors. I went to the door and no one was there, so I thought I was tripping. It was a card slid down inside the screen door from DHS for me to call. My suns first meconium was tested and found positive for THC. I had to deal with random visits and drug test to my home.

I could not eat or drink anything when I was pregnant. Meat completely turned my stomach, and I would throw milk up through my nostrils. I had to smoke to have an appetite. Von didn't want me to but if I didn't, I would cry feeling like something was wrong because I wasn't feeding my unborn child. I went through a phase of depression. I went back to school to get my GED. A month later I received my CNA certificate. I was put on the child abuse registry for ten years. Never able to work a job that dealt with children or nursing homes anymore. I had to change my major.

I told you I missed the old
days and that nowadays
are better

But I love you so much it
seems I'll be trying to get
it across forever

I told you I loved you and
want to be with you for the
rest of my life

I knew without a doubt
you love me and years
maybe soon I will be your
wife

With each other and
Patiently Waiting I knew
we would be alright

I have to admit you tried
telling me knowing you
had mad love never knew
you could be so uptight

But still I ask myself
everyday why we are
together instead of away

Then something tells me I
have a mission to continue
loving you and prove no
matter what never any
betray So sprung I don't
know what to do

Like Natalie I'm going
crazy trying to prove all
this Love I have for you
Praying that everything is
just fine but still confused
and feeling blue

Thinking that if you hurt
me like before the love you
have is not true

I told you to get it out of
your head I was not going
to cheat

And once again baby
momma drama looks like
I just got beat

But kool ok alright
apologies accepted

I told you I was a good
woman and I want to be in
your life

And swore to you many
times I refuse the other
men I'm going to be your
wife

You said ever since I got
this tattoo shits been

messed up But just think
there would we be now if
we hadn't of hooked up

I can't lie there's no
denying I don't want to
think about being
anywhere else

I can be with Von the one
I love why would I even
think about being by
myself I love you so much
I refuse to leave even
when I'm hurting only to
make this work I hope you
can see how deep my love
is and just know I don't
take our love as no joke

So, Von I Aminah Infinity
says yes, I do and yes, I
will

Through good & bad, thick
& thin

Me and you **Together**
Still

By Aminah Infinity

SLAVE PATROL

I started accumulating petty charges. My mom's boyfriend called the police on Von one day because he and I were arguing. When the police arrived, they asked me my name and I refused so they decided to take me to jail. I was getting cuffed while pregnant. Going to jail for not cooperating and giving the police officer my name. The charge was interference with official acts, making me appear to be violent or fight police officers. I was making a name for myself. Like a real troublemaker.

I was riding down Jackson St. through a yellow light, when a guy was making a right turn. He only looked left to see the car stopping to the red light and proceeded to turn, without looking to his right for any pedestrians. I got knocked in the air off my bike. I was in the middle of the street until an ambulance came and rushed me to the hospital. Upon arrival I was approached by a police officer with citations for being in the street riding a bike. The white guy who hit me didn't have any insurance on the car he was driving, nor did he have a valid driver's license. He got a slap on the wrist. I eventually got a lawyer and the case was dismissed.

At 19 I slept inside my grey minivan when my sun was 6 months. I pulled up to where my mom lived with her boyfriend. Him and I got into it one day because he didn't open the door for me or. I was probably just mad because I was homeless. He tried to hit me with a mop, so I hit him back with the mop. I respect my elders, so I don't know what had gotten over me. I felt like my mom chose him over me, so it was some animosity built up. The cops came and they cited me for disturbing the peace. It is no self-defense laws in Iowa.

I got a crib shortly after. Von still had some issues, but I thought we were in a good place. I had an open relationship with Von. I allowed other women into our bed, because it's what he wanted. Whatever bills we had, clothes or anything I needed he provided for me. I was trying to make him happy. It was frustrating because I am the only one putting effort towards anything. I do the cooking, the cleaning, the laundry. The other girls barely wanted to roll the weed but wanted to smoke and reap the benefits.

The steak was almost ready, so I called Von to tell him to be on his way home. He never showed up. It pissed me off. My homegirl Emani came over, and she seen I was not happy at all. I wanted to go look for him and she was down for whatever. After bending blocks for 15 to 20 minutes I rolled up on our gray Van. We had two vehicles at the time. I was in the Bonneville. "That look like the van right there," I said to Emani. I slowed down as I got closer to the van and seen him with one of the girls I allowed into our home. *You got to be kidding me*, I thought to myself.

When he finally came home, I let him have it with how I felt. I was sick of it. We started fighting and when the police came, I was on top of him, so I went to jail. I expected him to bond me out but there is no bond for a domestic. I was pissed. The next day I got out we had a no contact order. I went home, and he was out and about. I needed to go to the laundromat, so I called him to take me. Instead of him showing up alone he showed up with the girl he had been hanging with. Our other vehicle wasn't working so I was already salty. I told him to go drop her off and come back,

He arrived and I went to the car. I was sitting in the driver's seat as we were talking and he told me to get out, and I just started punching and kicking him. I was angry. The police were called and back to jail I went. This time it was a violation of a no contact order. Upon releasing me I was told to go to the probation office immediately. Once I made it home, I was notified that they wanted to test my sun for drugs. They needed a hair sample. I took my sun to get his first haircut, so that DHS couldn't get a hair sample. They acted like they were trying to take my sun, so I went on run.

I wasn't going to see my probation officer or even going out the house. Not sure what they thought this is but they going to have to kill me if they think they are taking my sun away. I called my probation officer and rescheduled. A police officer came in and asked where my sun was when I went to the next meeting. "He is fine," I replied. Not answering his question.

I left and finally called the DHS people and let them know I would cooperate only if they allowed my sun to be with his half-brother. Von had other children before we got together. His oldest suns grandmother is a foster care worker, so they agreed. The worst feeling in the world was not having my child with me. To think they would try to put my black baby with people he didn't know. In the meantime, we are waiting on them to approve my mom house for him to go there.

My sun would visit once a week for a month. Von ended up going back to jail. This time I was done. I told him 3 strikes you're out. That was his last straw. A month later I moved into another apartment downstairs from my mother and was able to put that behind me. I was happy to have my sun back with me.

I was brought up on charges of conspiracy with Von for distributing drugs. He was already locked up and I hadn't spoken to him in days. As far as I knew we still had a no contact order. I didn't think it was fair because we have a child together. Eventually I was able to talk to him and he explained what these charges were. He wrote a letter to the judge explaining that what I was getting accused of belonged to him. The courts didn't care.

My child case lawyer said she would be able to help me beat these charges. It was a confidential informant who was showed a picture of me and he placed me at the scene. I was not picked out of a photo lineup. Then all of a sudden, she couldn't represent me because the CI was represented by someone in her office. The public defender that I was assigned to just so happen to be a racist prick. I could tell by the way he moved his trench coat away from my sun as if we had the cooties.

I couldn't believe this was the man who was going to represent me. I put in for a new public defender and it was denied. The next time we met, he told me I needed to take this deal, or they could try to take my sun away. Seeing as though they were just on BS with my child I didn't want to, but I took a plea deal. 5 years' probation with a deferred judgement and 3 months in county.

Why were the police created? Why were the jails created?

For The Love or Money

Why was I even born?
When my heart is in pain
it's tore. Why do I stress?
When I only get more
depressed.

Why do I depend on
others? Only to get let
down.

What did I pray for a
child? When I have to
raise him all alone. Why
am I in pain? When I can
just cut my veins.

Why do I rise every day?
When I don't even know
my purpose.

Why is it that my heart
hurts? When there is no
one to help mend it.

Why do I help people?
When it's my turn it's no
one.

Why do I love? When
there is no one to love me
back.

Why can't I just die? Why
isn't it my time to go? Why
do I have to live?

Why can't my heart stop
hurting? Why am I in so
much pain?

Why can't I make better
decisions? Why can't I see

that somebody cares? Why
do I feel all alone in this
world?

Why can't anything go my
way?

Why do I pretend I'm in
love? When I know it's not
love. Why do people
pretend they love me?

When they just show me
hurt and betray?

<u>Why</u>

By Aminah Infinity

THE AWAKENING

The club closed down in 2009. That summer I
hooked up with my homegirl Jen from high school. We
went to South Dakota. That was the big payoff. We
drove there in a rental and split the bills in half for
everything we needed. Room, weed, gas, and liquor.
We bought our own food. The last day we were there
we hit a lick for a few thousand in like 20 mins. I
needed to find another strip club closer to the crib
soon.

I was working at Wendy's and still dancing. The
only thing is now I have to travel. I was going to
different cities dancing. Most clubs were within a
couple hours so I would drive back home when I was

done at five or six in the morning. The money had started to slow down. I didn't like being away from my sun. I was falling asleep on the road and it made more sense to drive home so I wouldn't have to pay for a room. Some nights were better than others. One day I would make $500, the next would be a stack. This night 8 to 9 hundred, a bad night not even $100. I had started traveling to Chicago to dance. Arnie's strip club was just too rachet though.

Had to schedule to serve my jail time after my bearthday. I didn't like how I felt about DHS and Police asking about my sun whereabouts, so I asked my sister Michelle to keep him. She moved back to Chicago years ago. She agreed, as long as I left her some money. I left her the food stamps card, my financial assistance card, and some cash. Praying, reading the bible and going to church made me feel better. The jail takes off for good time. I got a lil gig working in the kitchen and was out of there in 2 in half months.

The week before I called Michelle on the jail payphone and told her what day I was getting out. When I arrived at her house, she was packing my sun bag he came with, saying how I needed to buy him some new clothes. "You didn't put him in daycare, and he don't have no new clothes. What happen to all the money I gave you?" I asked her. I couldn't believe it, I was crushed.

Rian kept contact with me, and we became friends outside of the club. He was a tall older white guy. He would do generous things for me. Come to the strip club when I worked and just give me money. Didn't want a private dance or anything. Rian smoke weed so that was something we would do together. Our conversations were always deep. I could communicate with him on a level that I hadn't before with anyone else.

Talking about stuff that I never really paid much attention to in school, like American history. Wars, evolution, etc. We hung out often, most of the time with my friends. Anybody knew if Rian was around, we would have unlimited food, drinks and weed. One day we were sitting on the porch at his home, in the country. We touched on a topic about how we are from two different parts in the world, and it was not possible for us to be related. I engaged in the conversation but gave it a little thought afterwards.

He surprised me with four new tires on my ford focus when I had served my jail time. I wasn't expecting that. Rian was married but separated. His wife was leaving because he bought another building. I was going through a relationship issue as well, so we touched on the subject. I had been dating a guy who would say nasty things to me. "You ain't never going to be shit without me. You going to have to go back to stripping," he would say.

One day he came in the house and started hitting me with his fist. He choked me until I blacked out and then raped me. 2013 I made a conscious decision I was done with that relationship, and dancing. Both were becoming a headache. Toxicity at its finest. He was abusive, and conversating with men for money made me feel like I was selling myself short. Butt injections was popular, and I wasn't doing that. Seemed like that's what all the men was after. I started working at a telemarketing place in the middle of fall.

When Von was first locked up he asked me to send him the Holy Quran. Then started writing me letters with the Muslim name Aminah. He been out for a lil while now. He came to visit for our suns bearthday with his mother, Mama Kasmos and his wife. I had just got off probation and ready for a fresh start in my life. Von and his wife agreed they would help me if I moved in their city. I gave it some thought and felt it was the right thing to do. I got a U-Haul and packed my crib up.

Mama Kasmos said I could put my belongings in her storage area until I found a place. I stayed with her at her home. It was so peaceful with great energy, and aroma of sage. She had a big jacuzzi, so I loved being there. We would sit and watch all type of videos on the internet. She would show me things I had never seen before, planting seeds in me. I was intrigued and wanted to know more. Sometimes we went over to Von house with his wife and other kids, but I didn't like being there. The roaches I could deal with but them damn bed bugs I couldn't take. Von knew how I felt so he would come visit our sun at his mom house. His wife didn't like that, so it became chaotic.

It pushed me away and I ended up leaving going to Chicago with my sister Michelle. It reminded me of when I was here before. I didn't stay long before I asked Rian to come get me. *If I only deal with Rian when I got back to Iowa, I would be straight.* I was in deep thought as we rode the highway. I had a plan. Mama Kasmos suggested I call myself Aminah from now on. I accepted the name as I arrived back in Iowa before my 26th bearthday. I filled out job applications. Got a job right away at one of the telemarketing places I use to work at selling CenturyLink Internet and Direct TV. Everything was cool for like a month. I was working and stacking my money.

Rian loves black women and always had some of the girls from the strip club coming around, and I didn't like it. I became involved with him on a sexual level, and felt it was disrespectful. The next paycheck I used along with all the money I saved up to get me a crib. I didn't say anything to him at all. I was still staying at his home for a few more days. He bought me a used Bonneville. I had the key to my house I was happy. He didn't like that I had moved out, but we were cool. We still talked and hung out.

I spent the rest of the summer hanging out with my cousin, having BBQ's and clubbing. Lil Durk performed in our city and we were excited. After he was done performing my cousin and I jumped on stage like some groupies and met him in the back. "I'm sorry for your loss, I just want to give you a hug." I told him. He okayed for us to get on the bus. I was too thirsty living in the moment. I wasn't pulling my phone out trying to take a picture. Happy to have been in his presence. We were the first ones allowed to get on the bus. Then all the females started coming so my cousin and I exited.

One of my homegirls told me she was chilling doing the remix to Chiraq. I love doing music, so I was very much interested. As soon as I heard the beat, I pulled up my notes on my iPhone and began my verse. Everybody was impressed, including myself. 3 of us was on the one track. We recorded it in a home studio, the microphone was hooked up in the closet. It was a concert coming up and we were signed up to perform Chiraq. I waited until the last minute to get my hair did and was running late to the concert.

My full sew-in was not even finished when I left. Rushing to the center where the concert was being held and sped through a yellow light. A cop saw me and instantly got on my bumper. I could've made it to the concert, but it was construction that cut me off. I pulled over right in front of the police station. I cracked my window waiting for the cop to approach the vehicle. I was in Rian pickup truck. He was calling to tell me he was almost at the concert. I informed him I was getting pulled over and he was on his way towards the police station. I greeted the officer and he asked did I know why he was pulling me over, I stated, "because I went through that yellow light."

I gave the officer my driver's license and the insurance card. He checked it and came back to the truck. Giving me a choice by asking if he could search the vehicle and I said no. He smelled weed, and wanted to search the vehicle but I refused, so he asked me to step out the vehicle. I told him, "the owner of the vehicle is about to pull up. I don't feel safe stepping out of the vehicle." As far as I was concerned, I'm legit so why do I need to step out of the vehicle. My niece was with me, so I had her to pull out her camera and start recording. I was pulled out of the truck and pepper sprayed. I didn't make it to the concert. I ended up in jail with pepper spray in my eyes while sitting in a holding cell with no water or towel.

Rian and I agreed to have a baby. He always had some type of liquor in his house. I took a couple shots and we sat on the porch and smoked weed. After a while we went inside his house and had sex. I left and went back into the city. It was like a whole other world. A week later I had a one-night stand with this guy. I didn't want any ties to the dude. I was on some do him like they do women, hit it and quit it. I found out I was pregnant a couple weeks later, and I couldn't believe it. Rian and I went house shopping and he bought a house in a good neighborhood. I picked it out myself.

A 3-bedroom 3 level house with a big full backyard. I felt great. *This too close together* thinking about the one-night stand. I told Rian it was his child because I believed it was, but it was also a possibility I thought. I had to be honest in case my baby did come out dark. We had a Royal baby shower a couple months later. I arrived almost 2 hours after the start time. My family came from out of town and all of Rian's sisters came. I wore a long blue gown with a tail and a crown. I really had a good time. I had to do 2 days in the county for the incident on the way to the concert while 9 months pregnant.

54

TRANSFORMER

If I asked you to name all of the things you loved, how long will it take you to name yourself? Fighting silent battles against myself. It was hard to say the least. I knew this wasn't my life, I wanted more for myself. Believing I deserve all great things to happen to me. Overcoming my ways, not just saying that's how I am. Actually, wanting to change my habits and my thoughts. This can't be all there is to life. Same routine day in and day out.

Working a 9 to 5 to pay bills and retiring at age 65. That's not the life for me. I have to do something fast. My only fear was being mediocre. I know I didn't want to work for someone else. I know I am a boss. I had to go inside of my being and pull out all the things that makes me happy. When I was little, I wanted to be a doctor. The kind of doctor changed over time from a surgeon to an Obstetrician.

A quick decision had to be made. What do I really want to do with my life? Ask yourself that question. What are your likes and dislikes? Make a list. Then work towards the things you do like until you can decide which ones you should pursue. Prioritize them in order starting with the most important. Get a journal or two, from the dollar store would be just fine. In one write down your thoughts, in the other write down your dreams. The thoughts journal will allow you to see if your mindset add up with your dreams. Everyday reedit the list, adding or taking away things.

A __Dream__ written down with a date becomes a __Goal__, a goal broken down becomes a __plan__, a plan backed by __action__ becomes __Reality__!

~ UNKNOWN

"Watch your thoughts, they become your words; watch your words, they become your actions; watch your actions, they become your habits; watch your habits, they become your character; watch your character, it becomes your destiny."

~ Lao Tzu

I have been transforming my mind and the way I think for years now. I joined a movement that helped me shift my thinking and lose some weight. I gained over 200 pounds with my pregnancy. I was exercising at a nutrition club called Mindset Fruition. A guy by the name of Rico started the club. It involved daily workouts and Herbal Life products, along with positive and encouraging individuals. Keeping a body weight sheet and mark weigh ins at the beginning and end of each week. All summer 16 was the motto. I had transformed my body and was no longer the weight, muscle mass, or body fat that I started with. The team would work out as early as 6 am, and late as 7pm. We went hiking and ran up a set of stairs that had three different sets to the top. We did dance fitness, too. I enjoyed it all.

Mindset involves 80% nutrition and 20% exercise. Eating healthier was new to me. I had cut back on pork. I switched over to turkey bacon. I only ate chicken and seafood mostly. Rico had a burger and fries on top of the refrigerator inside the club. It was for everyone to be more mindful of what our body is intaking. The McDonalds sat for 3 months without rotting. It was great times at the nutrition club. I was happy to get up and go there during the week. We played r and b music. It was no profanity in the club. We were mindful of what music we played because it was children around us. Rico would let me lead workouts somedays on Tuesday or Thursday when we had fit dance, a hip-hop workout.

I was in awe when Rico told me he had a few of us out the group who had been working hard a reward. He had us VIP tickets to go to Des Moines and attend the Be Motivated Seminar. I'm usually loud, energetic, and not shy. However, this particular day I felt and acted the opposite. When we first walked in the building instantly, I had a rush of a chill in my body telling me this was going to change my life. It was a lot of people present at the seminar. Some was there to get help with their businesses, while others needed the motivation and inspiration to start one. It was famous speakers there, and even the million-dollar man who started eBay, but I didn't know of any of them. During the seminar I felt myself falling asleep. I'm a night owl like my mom, so I would stay up late at night. I didn't have any more of the turn up tea in my big 64oz Herbalife container. I nudged over to my teammates asking her if I could have one of her lift off so I could wake up. It is a caffeine containing dietary supplement which increases the feeling of energy and supports mental awareness. The lift off have been mistaking for a condom because the way it came in the package.

My team was all sitting in the same row. We drove almost four hours away from home for this event. It was 7 of us that went. In between speakers they would get the crowd hype with music and dancing. They had vacation give away people were signing up to win. I went to the bathroom and to fill my water jug up from the water fountain. I dropped my lift off inside like you would do an Alka-Seltzer. I shook the bottle up and chugged some on my way to my seat. I immediately felt alert and was no longer tired. The next speaker on stage was speaking about writing a book in forty hours, and the tools you needed to do so. I was glad for my energy burst because I did not want to miss out on the chance to do something, I always dreamed of doing. I always wanted to write a book.

The guy made it very interesting and I wanted to know more about the process. He went on telling us how their company was the top food chain publishing, and about books they have helped other successful authors publish. At the end of his speech he told us about the different prices and classes they held. They were having another upcoming event in our area. The prices were steep, but as he continued to talk the prices would go down. It went from very high to affordable in a matter of minutes, so I thought. $49 to attend a 2-day class with all the materials included to help write a book, including a free book cover design. I didn't hesitate at all to get up from my seat and go up to the table and sign up.

Next, on stage it was a guy who can help you overcome your phobias. He was showing us a video clip which played on two big projector screens on the left and right side of the stage. The video was of him on a famous television show with an African American woman. In the video clip the guy Bob Cox, was helping the lady overcome her fears. She was crying about whatever her fear was. Out of nowhere he gestured to the audience asking who wanted to come on stage and be a volunteer. My heart instantly felt that feeling from when I initially walked in the building. I mentioned to my team that I hate tarantulas. I don't usually use the word hate but no other word at the time could be used to best describe how I felt about them. In a split second I had a chill come over me again. It made my body start shaking. Bob Cox said had asked who wanted to come on stage and overcome their fears of tarantulas. I put my head down as to not draw attention to myself.

I am a real walking Goddess. Honestly though where I'm from people would fight you if you looked at them the wrong way. I know I am everything to look at, so staring didn't bother me. I am always told I should be a model. "You're beautiful, you have some long beautiful legs," some would say. As I got older and started getting tattoos that dream kind of went on the back burner.

I just don't like when people stare and don't say nothing. I mean give me a compliment, let me know if it's something you like. Crack a smile even, but just staring with a stale face say a lot about a person. Let me know if something in my teeth while I'm smiling or a bug in my hair, don't just stare. I have the most beautiful teeth. I finally stopped smoking them cancer sticks; which makes my smile almost perfect. Five foot seven, with the most amazing legs one has ever seen. Especially since I started working out and toning up. When I was growing up, I use to be skinny. Not that I'm fat or anything, but my legs are one of my best assets, to me. My face is flawless, just like the color of my skin.

It was over five hundred people at the event, but I was managed to be chosen out of everyone present. Not only was my team sneakily pointing at me as if they were stretching, but people I was sitting around whom I didn't even know was as well. It was a thought, but I heard myself saying out loud, "Y'all must want to get slapped!" The strangers did not even know me but because my team was pointing, they knew I was scared. I wasn't even the type to fight or use violence anymore, but they did not understand the fear I had of spiders. I mean he could've had an anaconda or something that others are scared of, but yet he had what I was scared of. That was not a coincidence. I believe that was God helping me to overcome my fear. False evidence appearing real.

What is happening when we are experiencing what we call fear? We are experiencing pressure on our organs from improper breathing.

That next month I drove down to Des Moines for the book publishing seminar. The two day stay at The Renaissance Hotel would give me a chance to be by myself and think. Even though I could've invited a friend to come along with me at the Seminar for free, it was meant for me to be alone. That is when I am able to really think better. I barely had any sleep the night before, but I drove for three hours by myself that morning. Luckily, I had already put gas in. I did not have to make any stops, even to use the bathroom. It was actually a surprise seeing as how I was drinking my turn up tea, and lemon water. I drove in complete silence for a short while, just talking to God. The other half I was either listening to gospel music, or the Motivational speaker Les Brown. He was the main reason everyone from my team was actually excited to attend the Business Seminar.

> *"Good things are supposed to*
> *happen to me, write that down."*
>
> **~ Les Brown**

I was super excited to be taking a step towards one of my personal goals. The group called me Spider Lady, because everyone remembered me from getting on stage at the Get Motivated Seminar. I enjoyed myself at the book publishing workshop. Taking notes on how I can write a book in 40 hours and all the other important and helpful information. Eventually it was more money to go farther then what the 2day class provided. The voice in my head just wouldn't leave me alone.

My unconscious mind was telling me to whip out my credit card and give them my info. Yet my subconscious mind was saying don't do it. I mean I would have loved to get help from the publishing seminar. I was overcoming a cashflow, and I honestly was not in the position to invest so much so soon. It was my mom's bearthday month, Mother's Day and my baby boy 1st bearthday. I was ready to empty out my kids saving account, for a chance to work with the number one publishing company. It's not that I couldn't scrape up enough money, for this amazing opportunity. I simply believed I would have another one. I loved that fact that I even took a step towards accomplishing my goal by attending.

I was able to reach my goal by losing weight at the nutrition club. I helped out a few people who had body goals. My diet was completely changed. I completely cut out pork and beef. Started using ground turkey. Cut out pop. Drinking more water, smoothies, and herbal teas. Consuming more fruits and veggies. My skin was glowing even better than before, and I felt healthy.

Rico invited me to church that following Sunday. I met him at Word of Life Church. They had huge monitors where you could see the lyrics to sing along. I was happy because it gave me a chance to be moved by the words if I know what is being said. I reached my arms out and allowed the spirit to touch me. I sang, cried, and questioned a few things about God and Jesus. Church Pentacle is another Church Rico invited me to where I met this kind and compassionate young lady name Rasheeda. A teenager but an old soul, so kind with so much light. The Church was fairly new, so it had folding chairs. Reminding me of another church I attend where I was baptized.

After the service everyone did a quick greet individually. I was able to meet the Pastor, Rasheeda, her mom and siblings. Rasheeda also gave me a gift. It was a fortune teller that read, "God said let there be light." We talked about writing, and she told me she was writing a book. I was very intrigued by her wisdom and grace.

Typing on the computer that night when I arrived home a voice went off in my head to look up something in the Bible. I picked up my bible I had laying near and begin searching for a verse when I decided to look up the origin of Jesus instead. The next time I went to church I told Jesus I was ready for the truth. To be saved, even though I had been baptized and caught the holy ghost at church. I was missing something valuable. I asked God to send Jesus so I can come to him. It was like a drug deal gone bad. Jesus was the middleman, and I wanted to go straight to the source himself. I started questioning everything I ever thought was true. Anything I had ever been taught, about God and myself.

Replace Fear with <u>Courage!</u>

You have to develop the courage to give up who you are now to become who God has made you to be. Change happens over the speed of trust.

You have to trust yourself, love yourself, be true to yourself, to make an impact on yourself and others. I believe in you.

Trust the process and never give up!

*~ **Health Coach Antonio M**.*

<u>**Use this area to write your hearts desires until you purchase a journal.**</u>

*Here is my personal list I reedited daily
of things my heart desires.*

My Heart Desire

To be successful at becoming the #1 best-selling
Author
Become a motivational speaker
Leave behind a legacy for my children Become
better every day
Become a millionaire
Walk closer with God
Become a paid speaker
Learn the truth
One day get married
Continue to lead by example
Be obedient and continue to praise the Lord
Keep all negative people or things out of my life
Meet more business minded people
Think and grow rich
Continue to brand myself
Self-publish my book
Be wiser
Erase all doubt, feelings/emotions
Once I get on help my family get on
Inspire others to make a difference
Impact others
Empower women

Believe in myself

My Heart Desire

Become the #1 best-selling book Authors
Become a motivational/inspirational speaker
Be a great impact and change lives
Be successful and rich
Write and self-publish my book
Leave behind a legacy for my children
Be better every day
Walk closer with God and live in his image Seek
the truth
Think and grow rich
Become a millionaire
Lead by example
Believe in myself and my culture
Be wiser and stronger
Live by faith, not by sight
Make a difference and empower the nation
Once I get on help my family
Find my purpose on earth
Marry my soulmate
Meet more professional and business minded
people
Help others
Continue to build my brand

My Heart Desire

To be great and leave a legacy for my children
Continue to seek the truth
Organize myself
Walk closer with God
Continue to learn more about me
Help my children understand the truth
Be ready for war
Be the best mom I can be
Be valuable to my culture
To be fluent in my communication with others
Learn about my zodiac meaning
Teach the youth and empower men and women
Lead by example
Encourage myself
Inspire others to seek truth
Love myself with my makeover
Continue to be the light star and chosen one
Motivate myself
Live in gods image
Live in love and forgive
Live in her image

My Heart Desire

Embrace life
Leave a legacy behind for my children

73

Continue to grow stronger and wiser
Teach my children the truth
Lead by example and make history
Trusting God and her process
Leave all negativity alone
Meet more conscious people
Love my children unconditionally
Continue to seek the truth and have knowledge
Impact and empower others
Help my family understand
Become one with the universe
Continue to live in my truth
Understand the truth and teach the youth
Continue to eat healthy
One day learn about my ancestors
Travel the world
Write poetry to not feel alone
Continue to love my melanin
Keep getting better each day
Organize and prioritize my days
Continue to feed my conscious mind

My Heart Desire

Believe in myself, God and my culture
Make history
Leave a legacy for my children and teach them
the truth

Continue to seek and know more knowledge
Find my ancestors stay away from all negative
energy
Trust myself and the process
Meet more conscious people
Lead by example
Impact others and change lives
Become the #1 bestselling Author
Fight and sacrifice for peace and equality
Shop for African clothes
Become natural every day
Exercise more
Organized and prioritize daily routine
Be the best parent I can
Know my strengths
Eat healthier
Have peace, happiness, and joy daily
Distance myself from negative people
Encourage myself
Write more poetry

He doesn't even know I had sex with him
in my mind

Stroking my clit like a guitar is that really
a crime

I called him up and told him how I was
feeling all he could do was smile

Not knowing that these feelings go back
unlimited miles

As he stroked my lips like a violin making
my river flow

I realized that I was a volcano ready to
blow

My cat purrring and beating like a drum

Not ready to yet climax but I was ready for
him to cum

I know I'm one of a kind sometimes I
think I'm too much

That's why we had sex in my bed and in
my truck

Each time he gets to the finish line with
his powers moving the pearly gate

Our skin so smooth made up of melanin is
sexy and one hell of a trait
I imagined me licking up and down his
shaft
Thirsty to put him all in the bayou like it
was my talent or craft
No hands just a mouth full of wetness
He then looked at me and said don't stop
you the bestest as he kept caressing
Juggling his balls letting him know this is
my court
I could feel him reacting as if it was his
first time off the porch
His instrument hadn't even got a chance
to dance yet we were both drowning in a
flood
Our melanin mixed together like we were
rolling in the mud
Now it was time to part the deep blue sea
His penis still hard standing tall like a tree

He reached in the water and felt
watermelon

My melons breezed across his chest like a
breath of fresh air

The pain his heart has felt I just want to
repair

Loving you because true love for a King
from a Queen is rare

I was In The sky floating high through the
roof past the ceiling

What we were about to do next I couldn't
even imagine the feeling

Exercising doing reps of squats he noticed
it was like an ocean

His lips felt so soft big and juicy like juicy
fruit I thought I was the patient

Visualizing his body like he was in the
matrix seeing things ancient

I didn't put voodoo on him but this
moochie is a potion

It healed him with just one dab Now he
comes often to the lab

He stays full of vegetables and fruit and
it's all organic

I told him he would be in awe cuz I'm the
best on the planet

Key in my piano the same as the tone of
his voice

As He tells me he loves me my body
started to earthquake I had no other
choice

I wasn't expecting that, but his heart
whispered namaste

I knew we were a king and Queen
realizing I wanted more than just a taste

My feeling echoed to him making him
burst raindrops all over my lake

Laying there fully aware and awake

Seeing us together physically damn we're
both Fine

Blushing at him like

He don't even know I just had sex with him in my mind by Aminah Infinity

HEART OF ME

God is not a gender, but an energy that is within us. A Godly frequency that we can use to tap into our souls' mission. This is just the beginning of my new life. Vibrating higher and higher into a new dimension. Matter is energy. E=mc^2; Energy equals mass times the speed of light squared. Energy cannot be destroyed; it can only be transformed. It wasn't until I isolated myself and start researching heavy that I became aware.

I started tuning in to more knowledge of self. I found out that the first human to ever exist was a black woman named Lucy. It reminded me of the movie Lucy, where she could only see at a 1% level. My mentor Mama Kasmos told me about a website called Rvbeypublications.com., which would help me on my journey. It has information about nationality, identification cards, and tons of other important information. The website helped me to know more about myself as far as my rights, and citizenship.

I decided to have a full lotus birth with my pregnancy. Lotus birth is where you keep the placenta attached until it naturally falls off. Scrolling down Facebook one day, and this guy that went by the name of Stevie Jordan had photos of his sun. The baby was attached to the placenta, and the cord was hanging from the baby to a bag. I thought that was pretty amazing. I had never seen or heard of nothing like this before. Doing research made me aware that it was the most important thing for the baby. All the nutrients and stem blood cells were going straight to the baby, and not being cut off right away like at the hospital. It is some women who choose to go through the process of eating their placenta in a pill. The placenta is then steamed and encapsulated.

It was a nice warm day, a little over 60 degrees. I had already been dilated 3cm for days and was outside walking to help with my labor. On the way home I felt contractions. Timing them to see how far apart they are. Had to be sure if it was time, before I call the midwives and tell them to be on the way. As soon as I made it back from the park, I started cooking dinner. It was just a little after 5 o'clock. I made a box of Zatarain's red beans and rice and jiffy mix cornbread.

The contractions were closer and closer, so I called Joan. She called up her crew and they all headed over. The wind was blowing in a way that it was communicating with me. *It's Time,* it whispered. My labor had started almost immediately after dinner was started. I gracefully moved around the house. Honestly, I prepared myself for this moment. Placing big candles in places I wanted them to go. Natural light was how I pictured this scene if it was at night, with me as the first energy she feels. No artificial lights would be used, and no other hands would be touching my child entering into this 3D dimension. Not knowing what type of energy, the doctors at the hospital dealing with. Dinner was done.

The midwives arrived and immediately set up on the wood table in the dining room. I went upstairs to take a shower and took some deep breaths to adjust and gather myself. I know the importance of breastfeeding and was excited to nurse my baby. The wind was still outside whistling as the clock moved. It was getting darker out. The contractions were getting closer and closer. Her dad was not there. He didn't really agree with my decision of how I was giving birth, so he was not included in the delivery. This was a peaceful moment for me, and baby. I wasn't tolerating any low vibrations. He was worried what if something happens. Completely sure, this was the best thing for us. I just wanted to be alone.

One of the midwives made me a Minnie Mouse Lotus birth bag. I just got the fabric from Walmart. They had soothing meditation music playing, and it was dark. The candles were all giving off the natural light. One reads Serenity. I was a pro at giving birth, all of my deliveries were with no epidurals, or pain medication at all. As the contractions sped up and got closer together my pace slowed down, and I started performing deep breathing techniques. I was bent over one of my couches that was pushed up against the wall by the bay window, wind still whistling. I reached out my arm as to be pushing the couch further. It was comforting to do every time a contraction came. One of the midwives started rubbing my back.

The tub temperature was good, and it was time for me to get in. It was perfect timing, because the contractions weren't letting up. Women know about that breath you get, that release you get in between the contractions. I stepped down in it and submerged my entire stomach in there and kneeled. The midwife was in my face telling me, "You're doing fine. It's ok." I promise if I wouldn't have prepared mentally for this moment, I would've been ready to snap on here she was in my face being nice like the shit didn't hurt.

I climber over into the whirlpool and not even a minute later I said, "she is coming." I was ready to push. Joan instructed me to put my hand down between my legs, and I immediately felt her head, and hair. I kneeled in the water and felt the top of her head. I took another deep breath and I start pulling my princess out of my yoni. The sirens and all our phones were going off, it was a tornado warning at the time of her coming through my portal. Sitting down on the mini step inside the whirlpool, holding her. Her father knocked on the door a few seconds after she was born.

I sat down with her cradled out in front of me as I began speaking soothing words to her because she was crying. I felt the placenta come out of my yoni. Water bag still intact. I moved to the couch after a few minutes with *Heart of Me* in my arms. Joan weighed her and passed her right back to me to begin breastfeeding. The midwives told me they would come back tomorrow.

They arrived the next day and starting catering to whatever, I needed. I had herbal tea, fresh fruit, and they even ran me some bath water with fresh herbs in it. I allowed the vernix caseosa to stay on my daughter for the first 24 hours. It acts as a moisturizer to protect baby from any infections. I placed the placenta in the tub with me and baby inside a red bowl. I rinsed it really good to get the blood off as much as I could. After the bath I placed the placenta inside of the Lotus birth bag, with a bed liner and some herbs. I changed the linen daily and added fresh sea salt and rosemary to keep the smell at bay. It was actually a pleasant earthly smell. Joan had taken the time to print out my daughters' natal chart and gave me a few books to read. The midwives wrote up the birth and went to the bank and got it notarized. I have an I was born at home birth certificate that they signed. I purchased from the Cascade website where I purchased a few other home birth items from. My sun stayed home from school and we had no visitors until after her navel cord fell off in 9 days on her father's bearthday. I took her to the pediatrician because it allowed me to have 3 pieces of paperwork with her name on it.

The reason I decided to do this particular bearth different is because I am aware the importance of it all. I am breaking generational curses. Going back to the way things originated from. A birth certificate is nothing more than an instrument established by a corporation. At the hospitals signing the birth certificate is signing over your rights as the mother to the child you just carried in your womb. Agreeing to allow your child to work(slave). A person who works very hard without proper remuneration. Doctors get paid big fat checks to vaccinate your child. To shoot poison in them. Vaccinations cause Autism, ADHD, SIDS, etc. Not to mention the forceful ways babies are delivered. Forced out the womb with things like forceps and c-sections. The wombman's body is made for this. A social security number is an account number. The Federal Reserve banks are a corporation which hold stock(you) and earn dividends. The placenta is supposedly held for cord banking if your child was to ever get sick, but it is never needed. It is used to help people in Government prologue their existence. The human placenta is the tree of life. **WE** are nature. ***The PLACENTA is the only ORGAN known to mankind that you***

CANNOT duplicate. I buried my placenta in my backyard giving it back to nature.

Why you and your partner should have a Lotus Birth? ***See Benefits Below***

Benefits

Reduces the risk of infections
Iron deficiency prevention
Transfusion of full nutrient rich blood cells
Contains stem cells
New breathing function
Enhances emotional wellbeing
Strengths immune system
Reduction of birth trauma
Increased supply of oxygen

Better parenting bond

Delayed cord clamping for up to 15 minutes can help the baby as well. I recommend a full lotus birth for a happier, healthier, more developed baby.

If you are pregnant or planning to have a child, it would be beneficial to write out a birth plan.

Ladies remember we are the ones the creator has chosen as a portal to bring the child from one realm to another. **<u>Protect our children.</u>**

I don't need a man to protect me I want a King to protect his Queen

You know like they protect their phones or their bros from theeeiirrrrrr woman...when they out being hoes

Cuz see protection is something a lot of people take for granted

Like the time when me and my baby daddy and his wife was out of town stranded

I got us out that jam and then I kept it pushing

Like our 98 Bonnie when he did all of what was on the dash and we didn't get in one smash

I loved that, and I still love that car And I'd still die for him today like there is no tomorrow

See today no one realizes just how important the woman is

No matter your skin tone we all one race from within

If it's not authentic its synthetic if it's not natural, it's fake

Sitting outside viewing my beauty thinking this here fate

Taking away from the truth at an enormous rate

But wait

Tell me what man can ever beat a woman

You never know when she coming you don't get a heads up when to start running

As above so below and When it rains it pours

Lack of sex and sunlight will clog your pores leave you sore because you need to balance the feminine energy

The woman is the key to the puzzle and yes, we got the remedy

We make a sacrifice every day for your needs

Some will be your trap queen and take a charge if it means you being free or have a threesome even if it makes our heart bleed

Have a child when you're not quite ready to be a
king because you still want to be a little boy

Now a single mother because you lacked giving joy

But boy let me tell y'all about the time I went to jail
for a traffic stop

I had at least 15 bags of weed in that damn holding
cell

It was just Reggie, so it barely had a smell

The point is I can protect myself

But I want you to protect me

Like I protect you every time we get pulled over, I
stuff the drugs in my crouch

Hold on world I'm about to turn it up a notch

Shooting down obstacles without a Glock

Living on borrowed time no Rolex no tick tock

They put the men against the women and this
fighting has to stop

Protect me like the pad when I'm on my period

I know that sound gross, but this hate shit got me
furious

Like the next generation don't need the knowledge
we are abusing Which GOD you chosen?

Is it the one that's outside of your physical
existence?

Or the one that gave you birth

Is it the one you were taught to worship or the one
who fed you first?

The one who died for our sins or the one who died
giving birth

From her nipples came milk that cow's milk a curse

Does she not produce your children? you know
what? don't answer that

It's obvious a man having a baby and her story don't
exactly match

The truth that is about who we really are

The truth about the different continents like mars

This not a song but it got bars

Huh

Yea I know but the proof is in the pudding

Men always telling you what you should and shouldn't

Well how about you shouldn't sag your pants like you want something going up your butt

You shouldn't sell drugs because you'll get caught up in the system

You shouldn't put your hands on a woman no you shouldn't beat her slap her pull her hair spit on her disrespect her degrade her misuse her mistreat her nor abuse her mentally physically or emotionally

When you cut me down you really only cutting yourself

When In all actuality it was me the woman who nurtured you back to health

Went into my bank account and altered my wealth

Just like when we have a sacred energy xchange and alter our DNA

94

And think it's ok to not sacrifice things to have it our way

Who are you fooling? weather my skirt is high or low it'll have you drooling

The best thing to do around bees is to relax

I AM the Queen bee you are my honey and that's a fact

I will provide you with all of the things that you possibly lack

All I need to know is do you have my back

It's hard trying to make ends meet and they not meeting but when you got someone on your team that can help you fulfill your dreams don't act as if though she is not needed

If that's the case Bruh like Mj just beat it

Keep playing tough and call J Lo when you for sure you had enough

Of acting pretending and playing

That you don't need a woman is all that I'm saying

Loving you unconditionally letting you lead eventually if you are caring for her genuinely you may just get a home cooked meal

What you won't do a real King will

She will take your dirty money invest it in a business and make it clean

Stroking your ego helping your self esteem

When I'm the creator of the universe you been informed, I'm supreme

The Queen indeed I am I must admit

Until we are all re united, I promised my ancestors I will not quit

Just to let you know this not a diss but to fix and make you Kings commit

Agree be honest and loyal to whom birth this nation

I've been in my own world and it's not easy but I'm being patient

When are you going to realize Queens make the mathematical equation?

Of you and me because without me there wouldn't
be no you

My friends inner stand what I'm saying and by
friends, I mean a few including you

Protect me like your Jordan's or your dog we all
know a man's best friend is his dog

My point is I'm loyal, caring, loving, I'm a nurturer,
provider... so you know provide for her nurture her
be loyal to her, protect her Your Queens, your
mother, sister, aunt, niece, cousin, grandma, wife,
friend, daughter, if you have one

Let's not forget the main point I'm almost done

We've been playing the game that we didn't create
because in Chess once they have your Queen the
game is over

I'm the most valuable player you should want to
protect me Protection is respect ING every
presence of my ***Essence*** by ***Aminah Infinity***

KNOW THY SELF HEAL THY CELLPH

**_Religion is following the messenger;
spirituality is following the message._**

A day before Mother's Day, I went to the Healthy
Resolve Headquarters in Kankakee. Mama Kasmos has
been running a healing house for years. She had
planned to do a cleansing ritual that would start my
healing process. We were setting up at 6 am and ready
to begin at 7. Myrrh, white sage Blanco, lavender oil,
black seed oil and avocado oil were used in the ritual. I
stood in the tub with my feet apart in the holy water.
Mama Kasmos gave me a sunflower staff to hold in my

hands and I started speaking in tongues. (Corinthians 12:28)

Then she used her Ka powers and touched my body all over with the sunflower staff for about 30 mins as I continued to speak in a language that I didn't know. I laid in the tub and was dipped in the water to activate the truth and language of my ancestors. When I stepped out the tub, I was given the oils to rub on the bottom of my feet for a new path. I went to meditate after and was able to research the meaning of oils used.

Lavender-color of growth, spirit medicine to pour out divine mother energy in essence of the unknown. Ready to nurture mind, body and spirit.

Avocado-used for love and money.

Black Seed-for production, fertility. Heal womb from any **dis-ease**.

When I arrived back in town, I drove to the dollar tree to get brand new journals. Mama Kasmos told me to write things down. I felt so magical after that cleansing ritual. Watching the movie salt with Angelina Jolie and they mention KA. Everything was making a lot of sense. I went from questioning Jesus to KA Power.

I always believed in God; I always knew I would get on *"Noah's Ark."* I used my common sense to question if we had gold and come from Royalty, how the hell did we get on the bottom of the food chain. I was led to KA. The Life force of spirit. I was so excited I went to the river to meditate instead of going home.

The view is so beautiful. Myself; one of my many selves. Feeling myself blowing. Watching the birds fly high and low. The baby ones flying keeping up with their parents. I chuckled at how cute they are. The trees across the river standing tall with lots of branches. The many generations that aren't quite different, but all one. Created from the wholeness of it all. Grass green, nothing but green along the river for thousands of miles. Water flowing freely with many waves. Gaia blowing freely.

Gaia is one of the first Goddesses that I resonated with. She was born into the Cosmos out of primordial chaos. Chaos is the formless matter(nothingness) that have existed before things came into beings. She is the mother of Earth in Greek mythology. The mother and wife of Uranus. This is just the beginning of my new life. Vibrating higher and higher into a new dimension. Matter is energy. $E=mc^2$; Energy equals mass times the speed of light squared. Energy cannot be destroyed; it can only be transformed. I used Gaia energy to take me to the next level. I am thankhful. Found out my life path number is 6, which is associated with Mother Gaia. 33 is also, known as the ascended master's number.

Figure out your life path number by adding your date of birth. *Example: January 1 + 2+4+1+9+8+8= 6*

Then look up the meaning of your life path number.

The number 3 led me to a fertility deity and African mythology. Asase Yaa is the Ashanti earth goddess from Ghana. The 7 African powers came to me through this dude I worked with at Nordstrom. After that I started studying celestials, astrology, metaphysics, numerology. I couldn't stop researching. Following the signs toward the light on my path. It was addicting. Numbers were popping out at me from everywhere. Clocks, billboards, car license plates, receipts.

0-New beginnings/Creator

1-Stay positive your thoughts are manifesting instantly/portal

2-Duality/partnership/balance

3-Equilibrium/Align mind, body and spirit/ascended masters

4-Angels are surrounding you/protection

5-Embrace Change/transformation

6-eevaluate thoughts

7-Spirituality/metaphysics/fearless

8-Money/flow of abundance

9-Completion/Ending/9 Ether

Our souls do not speak the human language. We communicate with the source through many synchronicities such as; symbols, numbers, metaphors, visions, poetry, deep feelings, and everyday magic like love. The Seven African powers are a religion. Religion meaning there are many of us. One of the most venerated of them all is the Goddess of love. Ochun is a goddess of the sweet river waters who represent beauty, love, fertility, and sensuality. Shango is one of her husbands, associated with thunder and lightning. Every culture has their own Gods and Goddesses. Greek and Roman equivalent is Aphrodite and Venus. Hindu Goddess of lust is Rati, while her consort Kama is the God of love. Hathor or Bastet are both Goddesses of love in Egyptian religion.

Everyone starts off in the womb as female for the first six weeks. You are already whole. Finding balance will make one complete. Possessing sacred energy between the male and female nervous systems which communicates information through neurotransmitters in your brain. Every living thing has both principles in them. Like yin and yang, one can't live without the other, they simply coexist. Darkness and light. The moon feminine, the sun masculine. Selene (Moon God) and Ra (Sun God) were both out at the same time today. The way they shine together reminds me of sex.

There are 3 types of sexual expression. Carnal sex, emotional sex, and spiritual sex. **Sex is a ritual, a Sacred Energy Xchange**. It can be used to manifest and create things from the nothingness into existence, like having a physical baby. Healing yourself will allow you to become balanced within yourself so that you are able to see instant manifestation. I went to purchase crystals at the Center of I Am.

The ones I chose to help activate me for a successful healing process are; Red jasper, black obsidian, hematite, smoky quartz, Lemurian, African bloodstone and my bearth stone garnet. Cleansing the crystals with sage first, then I activated them with my intentions. I played my signing bowl before the 15-minute video on you tube. Lit a few candles and laid out on the yoga mat with my stomach facing up. I began by laying all the crystals on my yoni area. I laid silently at first listening and tentative not to miss any signs. A couple minutes later I began affirming; Peace, protection, stability, etc. I felt a knock in my root chakra once I was done with the session. I ate a bowl of red fruits; strawberries, cherries, red apples, and watermelon. *"I AM HEALED,"* I affirmed. *"I AM HEALTHY. MY CHILDREN ARE ME; WE ARE HEALTHY."* Learning knowledge so fast made me know that I am going to homeschool my children. Shine light on all of the many truths about our school here at the Universe.

Moon

Represents our emotions
How we protect ourselves
Self-care
Inner self
Habits
Mother and child
Relations
Personals needs
Reactions
Zodiac; Cancer
Day of the week is Monday

Feminine Energy

Nurturing
Healing

Emotional awareness
Intuition
Receptive
Right brain
Night
Moon
Cold
Interior
Wetness
Softness
Mental

Sun

Represents who we are
Shining personality
Basic identity
Core selves
Goals
Ego
Purpose
Vitality
Creative expression
Conscious will
Zodiac; Leo
Day of the week is Sunday

Masculine energy

Rules the left brain
Mind
Solar
Light
Dominant
Logical thinking
External
Hard
Birth
Active
Function
Expressive
Science
Initiating

Our body is a system set up to get us from one destination to the other, just like a vehicle. What we put into our bodies will determine how well the vehicle works. If you don't put oil in a vehicle it could damage the motor. If you don't put gas in a vehicle it can't run. Same goes for your body. For your body to fully function allowing all your systems to work together properly you have to take care of your vehicle. Make sure you are putting **OQ** everything. **Only quality**

food, only quality thoughts, only quality feelings.

Root Chakra

Power center
Foundation
Survival
Physical Body
Security
Oneness
Etheric body
Emotional needs
Grounding
Material world
Color red
Located at base of the spine

Problems

Lower back pain
Reproductive problems
Clumsiness
Poor circulation
Colon issues

Low self-esteem
Emotional issues surrounding money and security

Healing foods
Red or dark brown; proteins or roots
Apples
Strawberries
Tomatoes
Beets
Pomegranates
Red potatoes
Onions
Peanut butter
Parsnips
Rutabaga
Watermelon
Herbs; cayenne, cloves, rosemary, burdock

Sacral Chakra
Creativity
Order
Pleasure
Sexuality
Emotional stability

Intimacy
Flexibility
Relationships
Reproduction
Passion Money
Joy
Color orange
Located at the navel/lower abdomen

Problems

Hip pain

Infertility

Emotional imbalances

Creative blocks

Sexual dysfunction

Low self-worth

Lack of creative inspiration

Emotional confusion

Lack of motivation

Healing foods

Orange foods

Tropical fruits

Oils

Pumpkins

Mangoes

Peaches

Sweet potatoes

Oranges

Seeds

Nuts

Herbs; coriander, cinnamon, sweet paprika, vanilla

Solar Plexus

Will power

Confidence

Effectiveness

Purpose

Social identity

Boundaries

Ambition

Intellect

Color yellow

Located at the top of the abdomen

Problems

Lack of confidence

Eating disorders

Procrastination

High blood pressure

Frequent illness

Liver issues

Poor digestion

Unreliable

Angry

Healing foods

Yellow or gold

Banana

Pineapples

Beans

Oats

Spelt

Yellow lentils

Yellow peppers

Corn

Brown rice

Granola

Herbs; fennel, cumin, turmeric, ginger, cinnamon

Heart

Self-Love

Unconditional love

Understanding

Trust

Lack of self-discipline

Worthy

Balance

Forgiveness

Compassion

Pleasure

Color green

Located at heart

Problems

Fear

Lack of intimacy

Feeling unloved

Upper back pain

Lung problems

Heart issues

Immune system

Holding grudges

Trust issues

Healing foods

Green

Kale

Green apples

Avocado

Kiwi

Limes

Raw foods

Collard greens

Cucumber

Zucchini

Green peppers

Celery

Herbs; basil, thyme, cilantro, parsley

Throat

Communication

Sound

Vibration

Self-expression

Purification

Writing

Hearing

Color blue

Located at throat/base of neck

Problems

Inability to express feelings

Thyroid

Sore throat

Respiratory

Insecurity

Cold symptoms

Stiff neck

Impatience

Excessive anger

Obsession with materialistic matters

Low energy

Arrogance

Healing foods

Blue

Blueberries

Blue raspberries

Figs

Plums

Pears

Soups

Sauces

Herbs; sage, peppermint

Third eye

Physic abilities

Visions

Intuition

Decision making

Astral travel

Telepathy

Channeling

Perception

Imagination

Color indigo

Located in the center of the eyebrows

Problems

Poor intuition

Poor eyesight

Learning disabilities

Sleep paralysis

Nightmares

Lack of clarity

Healing foods

Indigo

Herbal teas

Grape juice

Chocolate

Eggplant

Blackberries

Herbs; lavender, poppy seed, juniper

Crown

Cosmic connection to God source

Universal consciousness

Enlightenment

Gateway to other dimensions

Wisdom

Detachment from ego

Color purple

Located at the top of the head

Problems

Migraines

Dizziness

Loneliness

Loss of faith

Lack of optimism

Fatigue

Weak memory

Spiritual discomfort

Difficulty meditating

Close mindedness

Healing foods

Pure air

Spiritual foods

Air

Sunlight

Nature

Herbs; smudging herbs, Incense, lotus flowers

"There's an herb for every system, every organ, every gland, and every tissue of our body. Mother

Nature has put medicine in our food."

~ Bob Marley

LEVEL UP

To break the cycle once must 1st be aware of the frequency emitting from their being. We live in an electromagnetic field where everything is energy. We are all energy vibrating on a certain frequency. Energy is the life force of melanin within our beings. It can only be transformed, not destroyed. Dark matter or melanin makes up majority of the universe. It is ubiquitous in every entity on earth. Responsible for our skin color, eye color, plants, animals, and more. Melanin is science, responsible for the hue in man.

Black is the essence in which all other colors derived from. In a supernova stars release energies that produce elements like gold. The universe is composed of many key elements such as carbon. Atoms fuse together to create our physical bodies, transforming us into light. Light is a vibration, a sound that can be communicated with the universe. What frequencies are you giving and receiving?

The 7 Hermetic principles

* Mentalism: The All is mind; The Universe is Mental.

* Correspondence: As above, so below; as below, so above.

* Vibration: Nothing rest; everything moves; everything vibrates.

* Polarity: Everything is Dual; Everything has its poles; pair of opposites.

* Gender: In everything, everything has masculine and feminine principles.

* Rhythm: Everything flows in and out, rhythm compensates.

* Cause & Effect: Every cause has its effect; every effect has its cause.

You must unlearn what you have been programmed to believe since birth. That software no longer serves you if you want to live in a world where all things are possible.

In ancient Egyptian Thoth also known as Tehuti, is a God of writing. He is associated with Ma'at, the Goddess of; truth, justice, balance, harmony, law, mortality and cosmic order.

42 Laws of Maat

1. I honor virtue
2. I benefit with gratitude
3. I am perfect
4. I respect the properties of others
5. I affirm that all life is sacred
6. I give offerings that are genuine
7. I live in truth
8. I regard all altars with respect
9. I speak with sincerity
10. I consume only my fair share
11. I offer words of good intent
12. I relate in peace
13. I honor animals with reverence
14. I can be trusted
15. I care for the earth

16. I keep my own council

17. I speak positively of others

18. I remain balanced with my emotions

19. I am trustful in my relations

20. I hold purity in high esteem

21. I spread joy

22. I do the best I can

23. I communicate with compassion

24. I listen to opposing opinions

25. I create harmony

26. I invoke laughter

27. I am open to love in various forms

28. I am forgiving

29. I am kind

30. I act respectfully of others

31. I am accepting

32. I follow my inner guidance

33. I converse with awareness

34. I do good

35. I give blessings

36. I keep the waters pure

37. I speak with good intent

38. I praise the Goddess and the God

39. I am humble

40. I achieve with integrity

41. I advance through all my own abilities

42. I embrace the all

Energy is emotions in motion. Make a note to check in with your emotions daily to rid yourself of any emotions that does not serve your highest vibration. A mind is a terrible thing to waste. Here is a list of core emotions to help you determine what frequencies you are sending to your mind.

Core Emotions

Affirmation
Anxiety
Apathy
Appreciation
Bliss
Boredom
Contentment
Craving
Curious
Depressed
Despair
Disappointed
Disgust
Embarrassment
Enthusiasm
Forgiveness
Frustrated
Hate

Humiliation
Hurt
Ineffable
Lonely
Optimism
Regret
Reverence
Scorn
Serenity
Surprised
Trust
Understanding
Vulnerability

Your emotions either lower or raise your vibration. The devil is not a person or a place, it's the energy you carry. Anger is the foothold of the devil and it lower your vibration. Love and gratitude are the highest vibration one can emit into the Universe. Some emotions that lowers your vibration are; fear, hatred, anxiety, and humiliation. While the high vibratory emotions are; Love, joy, peace and enlightenment. The high frequency wavelength activates many DNA coding sites.

The kundalini is a cosmic energy of creation that rest like a serpent at the base of your spine. When the energy flows freely up your spine it is called Kundalini awakening. Awakening to your divine purpose and helping you to fulfill your souls' mission. I used different techniques to release trauma to help raise my vibration. Kundalini yoga, being out in nature, cleaning, listening to music, stillness. I couldn't get my mind to stop wandering. Like a computer downloading information thoughts just kept coming. I deeply inhale and deeply exhale, paying attention to my breath. Every once in a while, a thought would come across my mind and I observe it. It went from me hearing to seeing memories of my childhood replaying like I was sitting at a theater.

Bringing up images and feelings of all kinds. I was intrigued to know I could see into my past from sitting in mindfulness meditation. Practicing meditation to help clear blocks from my energy field. Meditation is a form of awareness of one's thoughts, emotions, and feelings. It can be done in numerous ways. Other things that raise your vibrations are; sunlight, connecting with nature, yoga, eating a plantbased diet. It is beneficial to be meat free for the healing process. Or just go slow and do what works for you. Learn self-discipline by at least not eating things you really like. If you don't control what you think, then you can't control what you do.

Benefits of Mindfulness Meditation:

Relieve anxiety and depression
Help sleeps

Better focus and productivity
Increased compassion
Body awareness
Brings harmony
Balance emotions
Regulates heart rate
Increases happiness
Improves breathing efficacy
Helps control thoughts
Increased awareness

Benefits of Kundalini Yoga:
Strengthens immune system
Willpower
Heighten intuition
Better decision making
Opens heart chakra
Resilience
Connects us with the divine
Increased creativity
Clears blocks in energy field
Awakening spiritual thoughts
Brainpower
Reduce pain and stress Emotionally Balanced
Better memory

How do you become Godly again?

Stay away from people or things that lowers your vibration

Become aware of thoughts and emotions to vibrate high

Plant based diet

No fluoride toothpaste

Non-GMO's

Sunlight

Drink plenty of water

Fast from the world

Meditate

Breath

Exercise

Dance

No Television

Draw

Practice gratitude often

Do what make you feel happy

Forgive

Honor your intuition

Set boundaries

Journal

Affirmations

Self-care

Proper rest

Self-educate

Read

Love yourself completely

Protect your subconscious mind

Simple steps on how to meditate.

No distractions.

Can use a guided meditation or silence.

Focus on your breathing.

Start off doing 5-10 minutes.

If your mind wanders bring it back to your breath.
Inhale love, exhale fear.

"Our biggest fear is not that we are inadequate, our biggest fear is that we are powerful beyond measure."

~ Marianne Williamson

I AM feeling fabulous. Woke up in a great mood. The night before I went to sleep listening to sonic elevator, it's meditation music. I have been feeling really lucky lately, literally in all aspects of my life. Money, love, relationships, health, finances, spiritual growth, just so much abundance and prosperity. I have really tuned into who I am and where I am comes from. I realize I am everything and everything is me. I am the creator of the whole human civilization. I create as I speak, as I think, and as I do, and feel. I am the creator of my own reality. I had been doing affirmations and positive intentions every day since last Thursday.

I was planting seeds of new beginnings. So, I can see blooming flowers of abundance. We were just starting the new astrological new year, with the Spring Equinox. I knew I was sure to harvest greatness soon. Euphoria was exactly how I felt today. I felt that everything that I had been working so hard at accomplishing was being taking care of. Today is the 2nd day of the I AM Challenge. Lunamoon created it with a few others, including Asya Domique. I was excited and up late again painting a picture of Ochun at midnight. All the things I was stirring up, lets me know that I was aligning just perfectly. Even if I could not physically see. I felt abundance was presenting itself to me. I was attracting it. Aware that I am walking in the right direction.

My obstacles and blocks are lifted. I would have successful funding in my projects, and detox friendships. Your abundance flow is being affected by the people with whom you're spending your time with. Choose relationships or associations that are inspiring, generous, and supportive. Remember **OQP**. After I would meditate a red male cardinal would appear. He would always catch my attention by his distinctive chirps. I knew the angels were assisting, because I was asking for help. Surrendering to the process. I want to heal.

After my meditation I headed to the bathroom to shower. The shower water felt amazing. It was as hot as I could stand it. Positive affirmations were playing from my phone while I let any fear or doubt of me relocating wash away from my being. *"I'm going to live the life of my dreams."* The voice said from my phone. I repeated everything that was being said on the video. *"I flow with the stream of universal luck. I deserve abundance."* I continued repeating after the voice that was talking.

I spent about 10 minutes in there. I didn't want to get out. When I don't have any plans, I like to stay in the shower after washing to deal with any other emotions that may need to flow through me. I had already cried them all out. The water was just perfect. I moisturized my body with some 100 percent shea butter I got from Chicago a few days ago. It always leaves my skin looking good, smelling great, and feeling like a baby's bottom. My morning routine was different. I felt different.

Ready to finish putting my plans in motion. I had to make some changes in my life. My life not really all what it's cracked up to be. By saying that I mean, from others perspective. On the outside looking in. I mean yeah, I live in a big house, drive a nice truck. Have children with someone who is a millionaire, hell multimillionaire. But that's his money, his car, and his house. We co parent. I'm just really ready to explore life. To pursue my dreams. Network around like-minded people. Eat raw organic fruit. Be closer to the sun. See different cultures. Travel the world. Eat healthy. Home school my children. Aspire to inspire. Love one man for the rest of my life and have financial freedom. Grow. Spiritually, Mentally, oh and Financially!

Here is a list of the soular systems and elemental qualities. Based on the position of the planets in your chart at the space, time and date of birth. It helps you understand the many aspects of your personality from different perspectives. **Astrology is the study of the stars.**

Jupiter

Represents what we desire
Expansion
Abundance
Success
Higher learning
Travel
Business
Spirituality/religion
Finances
Growth
Luck
Zodiac; Sagittarius (Pisces)
Day of the week is Thursday

Venus

Represents what we value
Love
Pleasure
Romance
Art
Harmony
Receptiveness
Attraction
Beauty

Femininity
Affection
What we want in a lover
Zodiac; Libra (Taurus)
Day of the week is Friday

Saturn

Represents what we achieve
Structure
Restrictions
Discipline
Authority
Protection
Responsibilities
Limitations
Perseverance
Time
Zodiac; Capricorn (Aquarius)
Day of the week is Saturday

Mars

Represents how we make something happen
Action
Impulse

Self-projection
Ambition
Aggression
Power
Instincts
Masculinity
Zodiac; Aries (Scorpio)
Day of the week is Tuesday

Mercury

Represent how we think
Communication
Logic perception
Mentality
Intellect
Zodiac; Gemini and Virgo
Day of the week is Wednesday

Uranus

Represents what we are bringing into the now
Change
Rebellion
Revolution
Humanitarianism
Science

Inventions
Occult knowledge
Individualism
New energies
Breakthroughs
Eccentricity
Zodiac; Aquarius

Neptune

Represents what we imagine
Dreams
Mysticism
Obligation
Illusion
Fantasies
Addictions
Oneness
Zodiac; Pisces

Pluto

Represents what we are meant to do
Healing
Power sources
Transition

Life/death
Compulsion
Rebirth
Life cycles
Mystery
Secrets
Transition
Alchemy
Zodiac; Scorpio

Earth

Strength
Prosperity
Material wealth
Nutrition
Foundations
Death/rebirth
Feminine
Star signs; Taurus, Virgo, Capricorn

Air

Wisdom
Intellectual mind
Communication

Higher consciousness
Intuition
Logic
Masculine
Star signs; Gemini, Aquarius, Libra

Fire

Will power energy
Passion
Love
Inspiration
Courage
Sexuality
Masculine
Star signs; Aries, Leo, Sagittarius

Water

Emotion
Lunar energy
Peace
Reflection
Eternal movement
Feminine
Star signs; Cancer, Scorpio, Pisces

Your natal chart can be studied at **astrodienst.com** to learn more about the characteristics of self. It would be helpful to know the exact time of birth to ensure that the reading is accurate. The different zodiacs represent certain strengths and weaknesses. Knowing your strengths and weaknesses will allow you to change your life for the better by working on weaknesses using your strongest powers.

My sun sign is an Aquarius. Meaning my purpose have to do with Humanitarianism. Aspiring the collective in creating harmony in our lives and leaving a legacy for our children. Planet of rebellion, which I don't follow rules I make my own. Moon rules the emotions. I have learned with my moon in Aries my reactions were impatient and impulsive. I had to learn to overcome that weakness. My rising sign is in Pisces. Pisces is a water sign, so it is an emotional placement as well. Dealing with spiritual life and solitude. I love spending time alone. I also love being a service to humanity. Also, sensitive and moody asf.

Enjoy taking time to learn about who you are and the areas in your life that could use more work. After you look up your natal chart, you can use the next pages to write down your celestial placements.

Natal Chart Placements

My Sun is
in_____

My Moon is
in_____

My Rising is
in_____

My Venus is
in_____

My Mercury is
in_____

My Mars is
in_____

My Jupiter is

in_____

My Saturn is

in_____

Sun is how you present yourself to the world. Your personality at a conscious level. The moon is what determines your emotional makeup; how you react emotionally. Your deepest feelings and inner self that only few can see. Beyond your personality. Rising is the astrological sign, it's how others initially perceive you as; their opinion of you.

The astrological wheel has 12 houses, one for each zodiac sign. Each house represents their own characteristics. After you fill in this page for your placement, go to the next page and make notes regarding what's in your house.

If you knew the type of energy you were letting in your house (Body), you wouldn't let just anyone in. You have a soul living in your house. What type of energy is that spirit carrying in?

Home	Characteristics
1 Aries- <u>House of Individuality;</u> Self-awareness, self-expression, outward personality, self-image projected by others, and physical appearance
2 Taurus- <u>House of Concrete Value;</u> Personal resourcefulness, selfesteem, material security, attitude towards possessions, cash and skills
3 Gemini- <u>House of Learning;</u> Mental activity, immediate environment, interaction with siblings, communication, mindset, speaking and writing
4 Cancer- <u>House of Fundamentals;</u> Home, parents, nurturing, roots, inner security, heritage, where you belong, subconscious and physiological patterns
5 Leo- <u>House of Will;</u> Personal creativity, entertainment, pleasure, romance, children, fun, risk, love affairs and procreation
6 Virgo- <u>House of Discipline;</u> Daily life, service, self-improvement, employment, work routines, health, nutrition and duty
7 Libra- <u>House of Relations</u>; Awareness of others, cooperation, partnerships of all kinds, legal matters, lovers, business partner, marriages and spouse
8 Scorpio- <u>House of Inner Values;</u> Shared resources, rebirth, transformation, joint finances, debts, inheritance, anything taboo, regeneration, sex and death
9 Sagittarius- <u>House of Evolution;</u> Higher education, philosophy of law, travel, journey, the search for meaning, ideas, cosmic quest, religion and

spirituality

10 Capricorn- House of Responsibility; Career status, reputation, authorities, achievement in the world, recognition, public life, guides and taking power

11 Aquarius- House of Sharing; Group connections, friends, clubs, global awareness, social services, networks, harmony, wishes and humanitarian

12 Pisces- House of Transcend; Repressed parts of oneself, karma, dreams, institutions, self-sabotage, self-sacrifice, solitude, past and spiritual life

TRIPLE A

Aware that I am rare. I know I am different, but I had problems just like everyone else. Instead of being grateful of what I do have, I would complain. The tarot message yesterday was *forgiveness*. At that moment, I pulled out my journal. I started a list of all the people I needed to take my power back from. People are made to be used not misused. So instead of letting others turn my heart cold, I took control of my life. I knew I had to let go of my old self completely to vibrate higher.

Old friends, old habits, old ways of thinking, or anything that was not helping me to ascend. Even if it was my own energies, it needed to be gone. God protect me from myself, I can handle my enemies. I had to learn to protect me. Not just physically but spiritually and mentally as well, my heart, and my inner being. Protect myself from my own self sabotage.

Overcoming my fears consisted of me being in solitude away from others to learn my energy. My own thoughts and emotions. I had to be alone to ache from things I couldn't talk about with others. It became a depression for a while.

I was walking around like everything was cool, but I was hurting, and nobody can save me but me. My soul was crying on the inside, but on the surface, you would see a smile or hear laughing to keep me from crying. I was unaware I was simultaneously allowing myself to speak against me. As if I wasn't good enough, or didn't deserve whatever I wanted out of life, be it peace of mind, love, or money. Many years of education, yet nobody is teaching the youth the importance of selflove. Self-love is the best love in a selfless way.

We all do what we want because we have free will. I had become so accustomed to being taken care of, that I wasn't thinking about my wellbeing. Being mentally, and verbally abused and naive to it. I was on the computer going from Zillow, to craigslist, to the section 8 page. Didn't even have section 8. Was just looking for a new home. I knew it was time for me to start making my actions match up with my intentions, and affirmations. *I AM Emotionally Balanced.* Having one of my bipolar days. I AM aware that these feelings I feel will pass.

I have to let the emotions flow so that I can move on. Like the moon we go through many phases. I used to wake up and wonder why I'm still on this earth. I inner stand I have a higher purpose. Giving up is not an option. I have giving up too many times before. Only to look back and realize I was giving up on myself. Now, I am giving up on people or energies that no longer serve my purpose. *My Soul Purpose* is to heal myself from my past lifetimes. Learn the lessons needed to help me ascend, transcend and crystalize. All while helping others do the same by sharing my experiences.

Loving me first and whole heartedly is the most selfless thing I can do. The will power to be better for self helps humanity, overall. I know I am way up because I have been down before. Like I know what it feels like to be happy now, because I have been sad, too. I am healed, because I have been sick before. Mystikal said "I'm sick and tired of being sick and tired." I changed because I was literally sick and tired of my same cycle of low vibrations. I craved new energy than what I was used to. Putting others before me is selfish. I value myself and I am now doing what makes me happy.

I take *accountability* for my actions and reactions. Looking at situations that show up in my life like what is this trying to show me? Instead of why this is happening to me. I embrace what is happening for me. I've had my share of roadblocks, and obstacles. I fought, had thoughts about giving in, checking out. Rock bottom is the reason I never looked back down. I don't look down on others, unless I am helping to pull them up. I have always been a loving individual who always wanted to help others.

Helping others can be draining, so you have to know when and how to recharge. You can't pour from an empty cup. I am a natural healer so broken people would gravitate towards me, because I too was broken. I manipulated what it showed me, and it helped me to gain clarity in which areas I needed to work on within myself. The work is easier said than done. That stuff was painful to say the least. I am not trying to change anyone. I want others to be the best version of themselves.

Whatever you see in another person is, a reflection of what's in you. I see love, and light in others. I see healed souls, people who are rich entrepreneurs, loving businesswomen who are warriors, great nurturers, and leaders. Real men who are great fathers, soldiers, constructors and protectors. I use my energy to raise the vibration of love.

If I am walking in love, I can only attract love. Love yourself if you want to attract love. Helping self, is the way to be able to help another. Like on an airplane in case of an emergency, the flight attendants will tell you to secure your mask first, before helping another. We are all one. Be the energy you want to attract. The spirit guides are assisting me. I AM exactly where I need to be. Getting in alignment with this shift that's taking place. I see all situations with clarity. I AM safe in all areas of my life. I have everything I need for an abundant life. I AM genetically encoded with

Indigo rays. I AM Courageous. I AM Powerful. I AM Fearless. I AM Infinite. Listening to music on my phone I got up to change the channel. I love future but I didn't feel like hearing him degrade women. I turned the station on pandora and preceded to the bathroom. As I relieved myself of water, I looked up to the mirror and smiled. Last night I put some sticky notes up around on the mirrors in my room and bathroom. The one that caught my attention read. *"I Am Strong & Powerful."* I continued to read aloud because I over stand the power of my words. *"I Am thankhful for my family and pure love. I Am happiness and I have happy thoughts."* I set at the computer to get some of my book done. I read two more sticky notes. Motivation to not miss any days of work. *"I Am Self-love, Self-Worth, & Self Preservation. I Am Self Disciplined."* Was all that was written, but I continued to affirm. *".... In all my goals!"*

"Thank you, Goddess, for the beautiful outcome to this situation that worked perfectly for everyone involved; Thank you for helping me have trust and faith." I chanted the affirmation. Hadn't been out in nature all day. I quickly slid my feet in my slippers and headed downstairs. Once in the backyard I kicked them off. I loved the feeling of kissing the earth with my feet. I stood on the tree trunk. Planting my feet firmly, earth grounding. The weather had been really nice these past few days. I stood there admiring my art.

I noticed a red bird. It was a different chirp sound. When you are aware and open to receive guidance from your angels, they appear. Red birds have to do with a deceased family member. I thought it could be my grandmother. It also represents living monogamously in one place raising a family. The sun was setting, which was perfect timing to sun gaze for a bit. I felt the energy from the sun. I felt the download of divine intelligence transferring to me.

For the next 10 minutes I filled my mind with positive affirmations. I looked over my shoulder as I felt someone watching me. One of my neighbors came from around their garage, looking as if they had just been busted. I AM aware I AM rare. Others look shocked when they see how attuned I AM with myself and the world around me. Some are intimidated, others are inspired. That's my goal, aspire to inspire. I AM proud of myself. Standing firm on my decisions to follow my heart. Stay on my path. Being productive at the same time. My babies will know I do it all for them.

I don't care if I was broke. I AM not working for no one else. I AM Rich.

I AM Creative. Full of ideas. I need to relocate so I can flourish. Be Independent again.

At first, I wondered how? Money does not sustain me. We need it merely because of the environment we live in. Trees give us oxygen. We give trees carbon dioxide. Trees give fruit. Vitamin D comes from the Sun. Water comes from the earth. Food grows from the soil. My skin is the same as the ground. Mother Earth Sustains me. I am rich in love, and finances.

Everything I need is provided for me from the universe. I have a full-time job, and I get paid in an abundance of ways. Some call me weird. I take it as a compliment. I don't care what others think of me.

> *"You will never be criticized by someone who is doing more than you. You will only be criticized by someone who is doing less than you. Remember that."*
> *~ Nipsey Hussle*

I have to stay self-motivated even when times seem hard. The energy we give off to ourselves, as well as others are important. What you put out is what you receive. Even if it is just a thought, especially if it's a thought. I set the tone of my day before my eyes are fully open. That moment right between you hear the birds or feeling the energy of the sun through the window, before your physical eyes can see. *Gratitude is my Attitude*, and I have that for breakfast with a glass of water. Love for lunch and dinner.

Positive Affirmations

1. I love my self and acknowledge my own self-worth.
2. Self-confidence exudes my being everywhere I go.
3. Others feel the love I give and receive it willingly.
4. Prosperity and abundance are mine by birthright.
5. I belong here and will fulfill my highest calling.
6. I am patient with myself and others.
7. Money loves being with me all the time.
8. God protect me form myself, I can handle my enemies.
9. I trust myself and the powers of my subconscious.

I use affirmations to reprogram myself to have better thoughts about myself. Awareness has shown me to take accountability for my actions. Aware of my thoughts and the frequency the emotions emit. Accountability allows me to remove any vibrations that is not helping me to accomplish my goals. Responsible for my beliefs and not what others believe about me. What others say and do don't make me shit.

Over the next few days take time to write your own positive affirmations.

Anything you say after "I AM," you become. Words cast powerful spells. It could be your qualities, your character, or anything that builds your self-esteem. I am Thankful for my existence, my breath, my heart. Being thankful is a positive affirmation to the universe. Gratitude is a high vibration. What are you Thankhful for?

Things I am thankful for?

_____

_____

_____

_____

_____

Positive Affirmations

_____

_____

_____

_____

_____

*"When the power of love
overcomes the love of power,*

the world will know peace."

~ Jimi Hendrix

LOVE IS

When a child is born, we usually look at time and date of birth of this new energy. The space, or city and state born in. The energy around the baby. The eve gene of the mother, as well as genes from the father. The grandparents or elders if still living usually provides the child with much wisdom as well as love. No matter if the grandparents are alive or not, they are an ancestor with deep rooted information within the child. As parents we just want to hold the child close and keep the child safe from harm. Upon arrival the child is brought into artificial light, in the hands of someone that is unfamiliar to them.

Within seconds of coming into this physical realm from the spiritual world their source of air for breathing is cut. Stopping the flow of the red blood cells and nutrients from the placenta. It's not long before the nurses take the baby in another room, and do checks on their eyes, ears, heart, breathing and limbs. Poking and prying on the newborn child inserting things into their bodies. Once the baby is brought back in the room the mother begins nursing or nurturing the child with her breast milk. The first sign of God the child knows and see is the parents. Yet and still the parents sign over their rights unknowingly.

The process of starting to experience or suffer from an ailment or feeling is closely watched over time. It is called child development. At certain ages in early childhood children go through psychological changes. Depending on heritage, environment, peers and schools. The child sees and hears certain things from others that is either helping or detrimental to their evolution. Children are introduced to a lot of things at an early age, such as molestation or death. Even things like vaccinations and when we grow up, we think it is normal. *But does one know what is really in those vaccinations they are giving to their child? The doctor can't even tell you.*

Puberty starts as a teenager where the child is introduced to sex. The schools are quick to teach about sex but not self-love. Set up as a daycare to watch your child and brainwash them while you slave at work to provide for the child. Meanwhile the child is dealing with different entities and their energies. Coming home with behavioral problems from other children. Before you know it, the school is calling you from work stating your child is a troublemaker, or bad. When all the child really need is guidance.

The child only knows what the school is teaching them. To obey and follow rules. To be a slave in America. The knowledge is inside the child, but it keeps getting overloaded with viruses through vaccinations that they have to keep up with to attend school or play sports. It has been done for generations the same cycle and not many pay attention to why their child is sick, or why they are aggressive and behave the way they do. In order to truly be happy, one must really go back to the drawing board of their existence. Researching the core of my being allowed me to see behind the mask of the illusion. I was able to heal myself. From generational traumas that happened before I was born into this realm.

Anywhere I go I know for a fact I'm shinning, with my five-foot nine slime frame melanin glowing. I'm beautiful with a Kodak camera smile. I have natural locks in my hair. I am intelligent, and very wise. I am very fortunate in my journey, receiving an abundance of cash flow and love. Most importantly my heart is pure.

Walking around frowning takes too many muscles, I'm good on the wrinkles in the face. I love smiling. Just feels so good. Any fears I ever had, or self-doubt is removed from my memory.

I love myself and I love the fact that my intentions are good. I am an inspiration, a positive, loving force of energy. I don't know who said the sky was the limit, because I always seemed to overdue things. Reaching pass the stars, to the cosmos. The Universe is limitless, and there are many possibilities. Life is a gift. My Royal Creations and everything else in my life is what I created. I am still always creating, with every thought. I am in a continuous flow of prosperity. Changing my thinking changed my life and I attract the people who resonate with the knowledge I am sharing with you.

Maat reminds us to keep our heart light as a feather. I control my life; it doesn't control me. I am the Master; the body is the servant. I am on a different frequency. A balance of love and money. I have been feeling so good lately. Ecstatic, full of optimism and enthusiastic euphoria. All of my heart work is paying off. Working hard on redeeming my heart. My heart chakra is balanced, and I see green. Something weird is happening to me, creepy almost. I like it though, love it actually. Welcoming the unknown into my life. A Real Movie. It's scary even because you don't know what's going to take place in the next scene. The suspense music is playing. My heart is pounding, and I am talking to the screen, like a villain about to jump out and get the girl. "Girl you better.... girrlll runnn!" The only thing is I am the main character of this movie. I am cheering me on.

Worked so hard to get me to this point. I am a star. Proud of my accomplishments and myself for believing in me. Grateful for my experiences, trails, challenges, and test that helped me to level up and go harder. An abundance of opportunities to grow. I trust myself. To make sure I protect my heart, I had to unlearn and reteach myself. The foundation of love, as I know has been tampered with. Like trying to replace everything good. Learning knowledge of self has been a long journey worth the ride, and I am just getting started. We can create the life we want.

I am aware of my power. I have written my goals down multiple times over the past couple years, but also take accountability for what needs to be done. As well as the action to get it done. Be careful what you ask for, because you will receive. Everyone has 2 eyes but not everyone perception is the same. We are all teachers, and students, workers, and bosses. One could learn a lot from me; however, I don't think I know everything. Time with self has helped me to appreciate life more. I went through self-reflection. Had to grow through what I was going through to get to where I am now. I have always been passionate about the things I want out of life. Living my life for me, and not what others expect of me. I have everything in my life that I have asked for thus far.

The Universe pays in numerous of ways; Gifts of Abundance, prosperity, loving relationships, healthy business partners, resources, high paying careers, good health, talents. My favorite of them all is air. Breath. Our body is so intelligent that it heals on its own. It breathes while we are resting. It warns us when something is wrong or right. If you pay attention your body will signal you by increasing or decreasing when around certain energies.

On numerous occasions I would give money away. If someone was in need, I would intend to help them. I spend money all the time on things of value. Basic needs such as food, shelter, clothing. I invest in myself more than I have ever did before. I preserve money for future expenses to further my business. Love and money flows to me easily and effortlessly from both expected and unexpected ways, from people and places known and unknown. I make money in my sleep. I have a healthy, loving relationship with myself and others all around me. Those who tune in to this station will be able to resonate with my frequency. I am not for everyone to like, but you gone feel me.

Love is a high vibrational frequency inherited from the creator. It is too big to fit in a box, and to loud to quiet. Shining you with its bright light. *Love; IS ENERGY*. You can feel it. Pure energy, the highest vibration. Music to your ears. Love is unconditional. A **Quality** emotion, an antidote. *Love conquers all*. With love comes a big reward. Having a pure heart pays big.

What is money? Just like you and I, *Money is energy*. A gift from God. It is a means of value to exchange goods and services with others. Money can come in many forms. Coins, gold, silver, and paper. What do you do with your energy? Do you give it away for a good cause? Spend it on things you value? How much do you keep for yourself? Whatever you do, don't forget to secure your bag!

I am the master and money, is the servant.

ABOUT THE AUTHOR

Aminah is an inspirational speaker who give others motivation to be a better individual for all of humanity. Using the power of the tongue to aspire to inspire. She has mentored Women who have come to her for advice about personal love relationships, career, and life itself. She has always had a passion for helping others, which is why she first had to help herself.

Over the past three years Aminah has made a drastic change to her life. In 2016 she started using products to help her lose weight from her second child, which she believes helped her get in a better mindset. She was supported and surrounded by a force of positive energy. Aminah became more aware of her journey by; eating healthy, exercising, and watching who her energy increased or decreased around which helped her stay surrounded with only genuine likeminded people, and release the people who no longer served her higher self. It became a lifestyle. Diving into the knowledge of who she is and where she come from left her thirsty for more knowledge. Being a Mother over all of Earth. Aminah gave birth to her daughter in the privacy of her own home having a full lotus birth. Keeping the placenta attached until it naturally detached and buried it in her backyard. That experience helped her to understand the importance of women, the only being able to bring babies from the spirit realm to the physical realm.

Addicted to bettering and healing herself through meditation, yoga, positive affirmations and rituals. She studies metaphysics and use the law of attraction to manifest what she wants in all aspects of her life. A new car, winning the lottery, love, and developing a new personality as well as her career. Aminah currently resides in Iowa. She thrives off the energy of the sun. She loves nature and animals. Her goal is to help raise the vibration of love on the planet. Giving ThAnkhs to the Holy trinity. Gratitude and love are the highest frequencies you can emit. It's a superpower, and she knows exactly how to use it!

If you would like to stay updated with all the great things Aminah has or be a part of raising the vibration of love visit her on her social media platforms:

Instagram: @AminahInfinity

YouTube: @Iam Queen Aminah

Facebook: @Aminah Gaia